Shabbigentile

by

Alan Morrison

For Peter,
With warmest regards,
Alan. M.

Get a job! Go to work! Poor, stupid slaves... Small wonder the world belonged to the strong. The slaves were obsessed by their own slavery. A job was to them a golden fetish before which they fell down and worshipped.

—Jack London, *Martin Eden*

First published 2019 by **Culture Matters**

Culture Matters Co-Operative Ltd. promotes a socialist
and progressive approach to art, culture and politics. We run
a website which publishes creative and critical material on politics and
culture; manage Bread and Roses arts awards; deliver cultural education
workshops to trade unionists; publish books; and contribute to the
development of culture policy in the labour movement.
See www.culturematters.org.uk

Poems © Alan Morrison
Montages © Alan Morrison
Drawings © Alix Emery
Edited by Mike Quille and Peter Raynard
Layout and typesetting by Culture Matters
ISBN 978-1-912710-10-2

Acknowledgements

Some of these poems have previously appeared as different versions in:
The International Times; *Militant Thistles*; *The Morning Star*; *Occupy Poetry*;
The Recusant; *Red Poets*; *The Robin Hood Book — Verse Versus Austerity*
(Caparison, 2012).

'Kipling Buildings' previously appeared in the Bread & Roses Poetry Award
anthology, *We Will Be Free!* (Culture Matters, 2018), and '¡Viva Barista!'
will be appearing in *The New River Press Yearbook 2019*.

I am extremely grateful to the Society of Authors for awarding me grants
from the Francis Head Bequest, the John Masefield Memorial Trust and the
Authors' Contingency Fund, all of which helped to sustain me and my poetic
focus during the period in which I wrote this collection.

My thanks to Mike Quille for commissioning the book and encouraging me
throughout its composition, and to Peter Raynard for his Introduction.

Contents

By the Same author

Poetry

Tan Raptures
(Smokestack Books, 2017)

Shadows Waltz Haltingly
(Lapwing Publications, 2015)

Odour of Devon Violet
(www.odourofdevonviolet.com, 2014-)

Blaze a Vanishing Revisited
(Caparison/ *World Literature Today*, 2013)

Blaze a Vanishing/ The Tall Skies
(Waterloo Press, 2013)

Captive Dragons/ The Shadow Thorns
(Waterloo Press, 2011)

Keir Hardie Street
(Smokestack Books, 2010)

A Tapestry of Absent Sitters
(Waterloo Press, 2009)

Picaresque — The Pirates of Circumstance
(chipmunkapublishing, 2008)

The Mansion Gardens
(Paula Brown Publishing, 2006)

Introduction

By Peter Raynard
Associate Editor, Culture Matters

In novels and films, plays even, there are state-of-the-nation portrayals aplenty. From Dickens to Jez Butterworth's *Jerusalem*, the rich and the poor are double acts on a political stage that is the United Kingdom. In poetry? Not so much. *The Waste Land* comes to mind of course, and the writing of such poets as Fran Lock, and performances by Luke Wright, tell of the political scene in different forms, historical and contemporary. So, in reading Alan Morrison's brilliantly titled *Shabbigentile*, you will be bowled over by the constant stream of anger-flecked images which properly reflect the ill-state-of-the-nation we find ourselves in today.

Titles such as *¡Viva Barista!*, 'The Battle of Threadneedle Street', 'Wood Panel Parliament', 'RU-RI-TANNIA!' and 'A Modest Proposal by the DWP', give you a clear idea of the mix of satire and political insight that much of the collection contains. His long poem towards the beginning of the collection, 'Not Paternoster Square' (i.m. Occupy London, St. Paul's 2011-12) is a good example of the slice and dice stream of consciousness description of this country as it stands on its wobbly plinth:

A Portcullis Corporation struts its peacock tribunes
In a coruscation of Ruritanian spectacle,
State-sponsored pomp that puts our Duchy
Of Grand Fenwick-cum-Camberwick Green
Back on the map of postprandial naps,
And travesties the need for cuts...

This is a collection about the lack of accountability and concentration of power in a country held up as a shining light of capitalism and liberal democracy — a country still struggling to fit into its shrunk-in-thewhitewash emperor's clothes. There are many declamatory poems which address this imperial struggle. In 'RU-RI-TANNIA!', this is given in the melodic refrain:

Ru-ri-tannia!
How can ya' now complain?
We'll make Great Britain Great all over again!

Such anaphora is put to good use in other poems, as in 'Thirties Rut: Clocks Back Britain' about austerity and Brexit:

Lies told for long enough become the truth they say;
Even a stopped clock shows the right time twice a day...

And the cultural references are as wide and deep as Alan's imagination. We have characters from Baron Rees-Mogg, to Noggin the Nog, Baden Powell to Enoch Powell, and the mouse that roared to the lion that squeaked. The blurring of real/imagined lines is perfect for our times — postmodern or not, the poems smash the pallid news of stereotypical skinheads marching on Washington DC or Westminster. In the aptly named, 'Drain the Swamp' for example:

Now white supremacists doing Nazi-style salutes
To Donald Trump, sieg heil-ing in Washington DC
Openly for all to see on mobile phone footage—
Not blue collars or rust-belt rednecks but dapper
Men in sharp suits, Hugo Boss wardrobed
Businessmen —self-made plutocratic products
Of the globalization of capitalism

It is they who are to blame for fomenting the currency of hate —they have their central casting foot soldiers, but it is big money interests who hold the power—some things cannot change when in the framework of corporate capital. Workers are numbers to exploit and influence through 'brand value' and the fetishisation of commodities, and in a brilliant metaphor, the homeless are pigeons, treated like shit on the streets.

Alan sweeps history up in many of the poems and gives it a good dressing-down, with all its malcontents of privilege and the harm and influence they have had on working-class culture. He calls for a return of books that properly reflect the culture of struggle, and which give us the intellectual grounding to fight fascism and right-wing populism on all fronts.

Now once more books need to be mobilised
Against the oncoming monsoon of moral
Panic and scapegoating, in the face of a new
Gentrified fascism, a bespoke chauvinism

It is within this book that the richness and inventiveness of language is used to such great effect. Skewed words, new words, old words with new meaning, all are here —taking them back from the right-wing capitalist media demonization of the poor:

With cloven hooves and "workshy" horns,
Striking Right-twisted attitudes
On plateaus of pack commonality, spice up
Copy till it's piquant with Scroungerphobic
Soupçon soaking up our lexicon

The state of the nation we are in, with all its uncertainty, chaos, pork barrel stomach-churning venal governance, is covered in this collection of searing poems. They are poems that will make you burn with anger but also with hope. Hope, that the richness of working-class culture, with its ability to get beyond conservative notions of a lost Olde Englande, has always had to adapt, so will always be revolutionary in ways the powerful will never be able to overcome.

For Vanessa,
Love in adversity

¡Viva Barista!

No one notices the poets muttering in mute
Pentameters as they sip cappuccinos,
Oval visages scooped up in coffee spoons,
Like cameos —foam-moustachioed;
Few of them have nerves for revolutionary views,
The politics of Castro aren't accommodated
At *Costa* (though Guevara's an Argentine blend
Finely ground as a goodwill gesture) —
Customers must choose between Trotsky and coffee,
You cannot consume two masters,
Bolshevik subscribers forfeit loyalty cards;
Baristas and Corbynistas rub shoulders
In café chains' centrally heated exchange...

Capitalism's spick and span in the polished
Many-levered silver Hydra, a gleaming
Meme machine, alembic altar-piece
Dispensing potent sap in a mystifying
Eucharist of alchemy and cream, worshipful
Suffusions and strange occulting symbols
Embossed on froth tops from milky outpourings
At the twirl of a wrist; *Precariat
Of the world, unite! —and percolate!*
Have a cup of coffee on the welfare state
Before it's finally dismantled into myth
Or picked up by the slate out on the patio,
Endorphins, serotonins, topped up while you wait,
Consumerist prescriptions, snowflakes alfresco...

It's not religion but coffee that's the opium
Of the people —French peasants sipped it for centuries
Mistrusting tea as a noxious luxury
Which turned the rich mad, so they stuck to their mud
Under Napoleons; and still today
Coffee is the tipple of the proletariat,
Most popular poison of public opinion...

Whoever would have thought that a bitter brown brew,
Arabic ambrosia, could come to undermine
Democracy, make us accommodate complacency?
Could Karl Marx have predicted capitalism
Embracing the bean and stamping its triumph
Through coffee-fetishism...? The West expresses
Its freedom with coffee in all its dizzying
Varieties and soupy nuances —espresso,
Cappuccino, frappuccino, Americano,
Macchiato, flat white— and endorphin-
Percolating properties that grease anxieties...

Ah! Kierkegaardian granules! Existential
Demitasses!   And the sweating barista
Is a living advert for individualistic
Service, for sacrifice of benefits in fellowship
For tariffs of the self —an embodiment
Of liberty in lubricated labour, Bartender
Of Arts, battery-acid libation bearer...

Common Music

The street-exposed splutters of the rough sleeper's
Acupunctural nap on homeless spikes —
Form part of the Common Music of our times...

The rattling laughter of the churchyard pitcher
As he drags at a fag-end someone cast aside —
Forms part of the Common Music of our times...

The broken tone of the sanctioned jobseeker
Momentarily tempted by suicide —
Forms part of the Common Music of our times...

The hunt and peck of the Decision Maker
As he puts his decision to sanction in type —
Forms part of the Common Music of our times...

The crumpled gasp of the unemployed opener
Of a brown envelope who dreads what's inside —
Forms part of the Common Music of our times...

The straining sighs of the wheelchair user
A "fit for work" verdict coldly defies —
Form part of the Common Music of our times...

The grumbling stomach of the coupon-holder
Shopping for hope in the food bank line —
The consumptive cough of the shop-porch spitter
Queuing up at the soup kitchen, tureen-eyed —
Form part of the Common Music of our times...

The hisses of steam from the coffee dispenser,
Contraption of worship with polished shine,
The under-breath curse of the sweatshop Barista,
Bachelor of Arts and dab hand at flat whites —
Form part of the Common Music of our times...

The plaintive strains from the pavement strummer's
Stringless guitar giving off sunburst vibes —
The gap-toothed whistle of the Big Issue vendor,
A windswept sound as if carried up high —
Form part of the Common Music of our times...

The dismissive scoff of the palming pawnbroker
Who offers a pittance for what money can't buy —
The sniff of the bailiff lifting out furniture
From the last flat on the street to be gentrified —
Form part of the Common Music of our times...

The despondent thud of the closing poor door
Shunned on the apartment block's cheaper side —
The glacial classical score on loud-speaker,
Vivaldi's 'Spring' looping on the PIP line —
Form part of the Common Music of our times...

The scissoring voice of the Atos assessor
Asking trick questions to disqualify
The broke schizophrenic by cryptic descriptors —
The mouse-click of box-ticking exercise —
Form part of the Common Music of our times...

*C*ommon *Music* forms a patchwork symphony
That no musicians perform —the people are
Its' unspoken composers, each playing our
Microscopic parts, as are we its' unwitting
Instruments, though none of us can hear
The music we make for water in the ears
That collects from our daily acquiescence
With the plastic splash of capitalism;
No matter how far we swim up, we never
Hit the glassy surface that would smash us,
So we stay beneath it but endure the bends
Of consumerism's percussive concussion
Plumbing empty depths, immersive experience,
Ego-submergence, ad nauseam, dehumanised
While commodities impressed upon us
Are depicted with human personalities,
Anthropomorphised, promoted instead of us,
And we are left faced with our alienated
Labour's built-in obsolescence, employed
Past our sell-by-dates, then put out to pasture
Incapacitated; this, the commonplace
Spiritual rape perpetrated by advertising,
Promotional spiel, copywriting, commodity-
Fetishism, pornography of the object,
Objectification of the subject, a psychical
Patching (incompatible with grapefruit
Like most fast-acting pharmaceutical
Citruses), it's not so big a jump from brands
To armbands, ghost orchestras tuning up
In empty bandstands, the baton has been
Tapping on the music-stand from so far
Back most can't make it out; and of those
Few who can catch fragments of *Common
Music* most refuse to listen to it —but those
Who do and dare to grasp its subliminal
Messages and press thumb and fingers to wrists
To trace the thump of its' ectopic pulse are
Forced to take tonics, pills or sharp shocks
To dampen unhelpful amplifications...

All await the strong-armed Conductor to come
Stamp his time signature on the blank-paged young,
Raise their arms up, slant their palms,
Hamstrung no more by inhibitions, freed
From *entfremdung* and its' distancing effect,
And from the need for pipedreams,
They'll march to the thumping tempo of a jumped-
Up Pied Piper portrayed as a product
Improvement to the politician-norm,
An upstart unafraid to call a spade a spade
(Even when it isn't one!), a demagogue, magic
Helper, hope-impostor who offers temptingly
Simple remedies to complex problems,
Brutal solutions marketed as miracle cures
With the quickness of quackery to obfuscate
Long-term impotence, a political spiv
Who mimics a *"common touch"* —camouflaging
Uncommon advantages and well-pulled strings—
That chimes with the memes of the moment;
The people will pound the soundproof streets
To help this Pied Piper fulfil warped dreams
Of power if it means full employment towards
A common purpose, no matter what purpose,
As long as it's common and purposeful
(But nothing as mass-empowering as common
Ownership: too much responsibility for
Most people); and they'll wear badges, armbands

And uniforms if so required —after all,
It's no different to dress codes of corporate
Employment; but their trumping boots will beat
In time not to authentic *Common Music*
But to its' brasher cousin, Rough Music,
A brassier fabrication that announces itself
With thrashing fanfares, cacophonous pomp,
Cymbals-clashing chiliasm, infecting
Yet cleansing, wounding yet healing, constraining
Yet cathartic, brutish but retributive,
Visceral yet disciplined, muscularly chic —
Contagious to the cauliflower ear— aurally
Seductive to those who feel disenfranchised,
Used, abused and left behind after ploughblades
Of globalisation have scythed through
Reducing manufacturing heartlands
To derelict rust-belts and scrubland dustbowls
Of obsolete industries; those who'd otherwise
Fumble ambitionless and numbed through
Make-do, cobbled-together consciousness,
Invalidated lives, deaf or indifferent
To muttering undertones of *Common Music*
That cannot filter through mufflers of ill-informed
Self-interest and false fellowship that only
Goes so far and invariably begins and ends
With family and friends but doesn't extend
To fellow citizens, the unrelated or unfamiliar,
Least of all strangers, foreigners, aliens;
And O those rose petal petitions that fall
On deaf ears: *"There's more that unites
Than divides us"* —scratched out by thornier
Rhetoric, snagged on barbed remonstrations,
Or cut down in frantic acts by radicalised
Maniacs, suburbanite extremists; now
Empathy's lost impetus, is spent human tender,
Political capital long-depleted —the bandstands
Sit empty, and *Common Music* hums faintly
From a distance sympathetically attuned,
Fragilely arppegiated to an angelic —
And Audenic— change of heart-strings...

B ut the *Common Music* of our times will be
The source of tomorrow's nursery rhymes
That will tell future children of tarnished minds
That closed themselves to the warning signs
Of what they were becoming —that thorniest
Twist in the national character that always
Threatens to rupture to the surface
In the most foundation-shaking circumstances:
Fascist —hatchling of the capitalist pact;
Reactionary rash flaring up against dogged
Progress; intransigent allergy to change;
Neurotic hunger for control; intolerance
Of choice; moral mange; itch for psychical
Anchoring; thirst for certainty; the primal
Need for a firm parental hand —or whip-hand,
Preferably; what Fromm portrayed as *"fear
Of freedom"* —that is, fear of freedom's
Dizzying carousel of choices and counter-
Choices, galloping vertigo that Kierkegaard
Coigned as *angst* —but a rugged, battle-scarred
Tyrannical angst, antagonistic; and
Its anti-rhythmic dithyrambs surface as
Rough Music which blasts the brashest
And brassiest, drowns out the tonic
Which some, mostly optimists, Communists,
Socialists and those with quixotic shell-likes
Recognise unconsciously as *Common Music...*

The Battle of Threadneedle Street
1st April 2009

Bankers launder taunts out to fry from glass towers,
Bolting back in to beat inflammatory retreat —
Here storms the battering ram of Uncommon People:
One hoodie headline-grabber hurls a hatchet through a window
Of the Royal Bank of Babel's vacated altars
Unheeding a tweedy elder's pained face
Blanched as a librarian's as he stamps his hand
On the air's malleable page, woollily howling:
"No! No violence —no violence!" But no sooner
Has anarchy lashed back after mauled decades
Of Thatcher's snatching mane, a booted bruise of blue
Tramps past cameras, trampling placards
And kettling protestors in a Metropolitan pen;
A hollow tortoise-shell of transparent shields,
Shin-licking truncheons and electric-crackling tasers —
Tsarists on the streets visiting a movable
Zimniy Dvorets on the rioting peasants...

O this nation of tsars and tasers, tasers and tsars!

The Establishment can be a battering ram:
A rampaging hammer barricading mass anger
In against itself until hedged-in insurgents
Simmer down, dumbstruck, sunburnt, spluttering,
Dehydrated in the brick-dust kicked up
Into aftermath of ring-fenced, incendiary heat...

Camels in flannel suits commute back through
The needling eye of Threadneedle Street...

Wood Panel Parliament
On the MPs' expenses scandal 2009

Catch the frantic scratch of pens in chequebooks:
The sound of Parliament dismantling —
Democracy's swine impaled on meat-hooks.

An electorate, betrayed to tenterhooks:
Each Fascist warming up at his dark husting.
Catch the frantic scratch of pens in chequebooks:

Woodlice crawl out from the smouldering nooks.
Pugilist grubs rub hands to dish a pasting
For democracy to spit and pop on meat-hooks.

MPs named and shamed for flipping the books.
The Speaker, transparent as wood panelling
Catches the frantic scratches of chequebooks.

A hunting of the nark by booted spooks
So no more moles expose blank cheque accounting:
Democracy's swine impaled on meat-hooks.

The match has been struck by scandal's Guy Fawkes!
Kliesthenes! Keir Hardie! In their graves, turning!
Catch the frantic scratch of pens in chequebooks:
Democracy's swine impaled on meat-hooks.

Thirties Rut: Clocks Back Britain

THERE are millions of people in Alarm Clock Britain. People... who have to get up every morning and work hard to get on in life. ...People who don't want to rely on state handouts. ...People who are not poor but struggle to stay out of the red. They are the backbone of Britain. These are the people who will get this country moving again. It is their hard graft... that will get us out of the hole Labour left us in. This Government is formed by a coalition of two parties and we want to join the people of Alarm Clock Britain in another coalition. A coalition of people prepared to roll up their sleeves and get the nation back on its feet.

—Nick Clegg, *The Sun*, 11th January 2011

"The Great Recession came about not as a result
Of rampant capitalism and banks gambling away
The nation's wealth, but because of unsustainable
Public expenditure and a bloated welfare state
That was destined to rupture sooner or later —
Now the boil has to be lanced and a little blood let
To pay off the deficit —but we're all in this together...
The burden will fall on the broadest shoulders
Of dwarves, so roll up your sleeves, heed the mantras:
No complaints, There Is No Alternative (TINA)"...

Lies told for long enough become the truth they say;
Even a stopped clock shows the right time twice a day...

"This nation was near-bankrupted not by a global
Economic crisis and a burst housing bubble
On the back of sub-prime mortgages and buy-to-lets,
But by the profligacy of a Labour Government
That borrowed in the boom and spent, spent, spent,
Bought off their voters with fatter state handouts,
Until the country found itself penniless just as
The stock markets collapsed and there was no surplus,
But the biggest peacetime budget deficit in Europe..."

Lies told for long enough become the truth they say;
Even a stopped clock shows the right time twice a day...

"This country's scourged by scroungers who mug the taxpayers
For benefits they don't deserve that are too generous;
For too long there's been a culture of entitlement,
Of idleness, of something for nothing, time to restore
The contributory principle; it wasn't an absence
Of rent controls which caused housing benefits to spiral:
Rents were driven up by benefits, idleness by rising dole..."

Lies told for long enough become the truth they say;
Even a stopped clock shows the right time twice a day...

"This nation's ruled by Brussels, by unelected bureaucrats,
We must liberate ourselves and take our country back,
Scrap the Human Rights Act which restricts our animal spirits
And entrepreneurship; cut red tape, strip employment rights
And normalise zero-hours contracts to make it easier
For businesses to employ more people at less expense,
And gift the long-term unemployed unpaid work experience..."

Lies told for long enough become the truth they say;
Even a stopped clock shows the right time twice a day...

"Brexit will make Britain Great again, a magical land
Of warm beer, John Bull, jubilees, ubiquitous bunting,
Where the common people play a part in empire rebuilding;
There'll be full employment, no more competing Polish hop-
Pickers pushing wages down, no more empty "jam tomorrow"
Promises from politicians; in this new dawn it's jam today
For the "Just About Managing" ("Jams") —and Marmalades..."

Lies told for long enough stick; "post-truth" we say:
A stopped clock tells the right time ALL the day...

Times New Roman
After the England riots of August 2011

'...that decadent mystique of athletics' —D.H. Lawrence

The emperor twiddles while London burns,
Bathed in Tuscan sun far from blues and greens
And feral scenes long-seeded by his inbred
Pedigrees' privileges and titled entitlements,
Brindled with venal greed petted to respectability...
Interrupts his holiday to swoop back home by
Private jet —a pigeon-faced cooing coup-carrier
With one big carbon claw-print— and take up
His plinth for prime ministerial posturing
Outside the black bricks of Downing Street
For a press conference to condemn *"sick"*
Pockets of his Brig Society and confiscate
Their dockets to diminishing returns, douse
Malcontents with matchsticks of austerities,
Arsons of fiscal consolidations, capitalise
On flames to raze stakes of cuts-gutted
Communities punished by his consulship's
Incendiary policies, blazes conflagrated by
His own igniting dogmas —combustible
Ballots for tinder boxes and Neronic torches...

The Tribune's harping sparring-partner Boris
The Hubristic sucks in his girth while comically
Hoisting a broom, attempting to buff-up charred
Residents of a blackened East End street
With all the gusto of a public school prefect
Signalling his fag to sweep up the dormitory,
No doubt wishing he was still in the air-
Conditioned suite at *The Spectator* rather
Than the toxic heat of Toxteth-ghosted Tottenham,
The thick of politicking in buy-to-burn slums,
Gutted doughnut ghettos' scorched-earth
Gentrification...

...Myopic emperors,
Hollow orators, complicit critics throwing
Shadows of their own choices onto riots
Grown from spouts of propertied rhetoric,
Only to shoot missiles of *"exemplary sentences"* —
Stones in glass houses of shuttered hypocrites...

All must be scrubbed, swept pristinely clean
And decadent for Twenty-Twelve's end-
Of-empire Games, replete with Paralympics
For incapacity claimants to compete on tracks
To overturn the hurdles to paltry alms
They formerly received to keep them in
A palatable tempo of poverty —sponsored
By Atos Solutions (and Maximus latterly):
Wheelchair races, high-jumps for crutches,
Javelin contests for chemo patients, spinning
Plates for the paralysed, discus deciders
For the mentally afflicted, heads already
Frisbee-spun on antipsychotics —all fun
And titillating returns for taxpayer spectators...

Then the crowning crowd-pleaser as rioters,
Protestors, anti-capitalists, placard-wavers,
Students, strikers and socialists are thrown
To red-top lions for a mauling to the roar
Of clamouring mobs hungering gore,
The stadium-cum-Colosseum erupting
Into choruses of *"Down! Down! Down!"*
Then the show-stopping pause while all
Wait with baited breaths for the emperor's
Thumb to lift —then plunge...O Olympics
Throw your crumbs and circuses upon us!
Unfold your sport and frolics on the soiled
Picnic spread of anomic Londinium —
White phosphorous scorch-mark at the gnarled
Scrag-end of an overcooked mutton,
An ice-pinched tumour on the Bow Back River,
Tory torch alight to ignite gentrification...

Not Paternoster Square
i.m. Occupy London, St.Paul's 2011-12

1.

All roads lead from Paternoster Square —
Project outwards as shadows thrown from
A crouching Exchange that pretends not to be there,
Where Exchequers square indulgences
For patronage in currencies of green benches,
Shadow dues spilt into coffers of costermongers,
Cutpurses, safecrackers and all the cawing
Ravens in black and red liveries, feathered
Beefeaters to a breed, jackdaws stalking
Craws of an ancient cadastral that saps
A cash-strapped Capital in spectral taxes,
Encrusts its subterranean arteries of punctured
Under-lungs with atmospheric residues
Left behind from centuries of symbolic ceremonies,
Occulting rituals, public mimes...

2.

A Portcullis Corporation struts its' peacock tribunes
In a coruscation of Ruritanian spectacle,
State-sponsored pomp that puts our Duchy
Of Grand Fenwick-cum-Camberwick Green
Back on the map of postprandial naps,
And travesties the need for cuts: austerity
Can't penetrate the Establishment, it seems;
Out rolls that baroquely carved coach,
Gold-gilded inaugural carriage for Charles Asgill's
Swearing in on 9th November 1757 —
From Alderman of Candlewick Ward
To Sheriff then Lord Mayor of the City of London,
Blip in plumed tricorn and ermined embarrassment
Of merchant bank and baronetcy
In the otherwise rag-tag ancestry
Of anticlockwise socialist Whittingtons

On my father's distaff side... That line's fortunes
Truncated abruptly, unravelled to bankruptcy
Of impecunious motto —*Sui oblitus
Commodi: Forgetful of his own interest*;
Draped to shabby pageantries of down-at-heel
Genteel *Something will turn ups* singed
Into nicotined samplers' dog-end genealogies;
Unproductive croups of pocket lined with chits
Escorted without ceremony; copper tonics
Scooped on rusty-spooned quixotries
Of polished thoughts for future heirlooms;
Furniture tented in linen palls to guard against
Gradualist dusts —mothballed in Fabian platitudes;
Ormolus of human flourishing groomed through
Willowing blood-looms to stubbed-out pit-towns,
Carcinomas of chronic Norths —sable plumes
Tousling to charabancs of Birkenhead clouds...

3.

Tarpaulins sprung from under St. Paul's spandrels
Like mushrooms in the damp: tents knelt
At the cassocked hem of stone-rumpled steps,
Covers for cast-off human furniture,
Refusenik-kitsch —a camp of linen pyramids
Flapping like képi blancs, or topee neck curtains
Of Sudan campaigns, reconnaissance to spot
Camels edging near Threadneedle's unhinging eye;
A crop of tepees pitched by rainbow tribes:
Anarchists, anti-capitalists and practical Christians,
Satinette affiliations, proselytising pigeons,
Columbiform relief columns combing vaulted
Alcoves of pitchforked atmospherics clung
To greenhorn Tongues strung by Glossolalias
Of cause-abridging slogans, bird-chant
Saturnalias punctuating apathies and plastic-
Card apartheids, thumped by metes-and-bounds
Of dog-eared buildings thumbed to grubbiness;
Stunned moles at a distance —but up close:
Badger-brindled Diggers, ignited egalitarians,
Militant tillers of asset-stripped light,
And dole-endangered Levellers —at night:
Truant stars, trick-or-treating scamps
With placards and wands of rustling sparklers,
A silent concert's cobs of swaying lighters
Sailing over waves of canvas; Robin Hoods
And bereted men in concrete forest clearings...

4.

Far cries from those cowed deciduous souls
Cloaked blackly in the implacable scum
Of dark autumnal London: Nosterity's
Moratorium, Dickensian chic of Pecksniff,
Quilp and Heep for bicentennial reconstruction...
But we *KEEP CALM AND BUGGER ON*
In Bakelite mentalities, out with the bunting,
In with punting, put the unemployed
In polo shirts and see-through ponchos,
Unpaid 'steward' *untermenschen* patriotically
Kipping under dripping London Bridge where
They'd been deposited with sleeping bags
In the damp small hours, conscripts of Close
Protection sub-contracted by Tomorrow's
People (*Exploiters of Today's*), to work on
Bank holidays, exhausted, wet, humiliated,
Rinsed of self-respect but made to forgo
A wage and flap Lilliputian flags of Grand
Brobdingnag as gold-dripped jubilee barges
Bling on by to choppy choruses of *Britons ...
Never, never shall—be—slaves...* (except
To themselves and their secret masters) —
True sovereignty on the never-never
In this tin-pot RURI-TANNIA where
Bankrupt 'subjects' trip over themselves
To glimpse an ermined family of ingrates
In flagrante who reign over them;
A floating court of dynastic parasites
That hard-pressed taxpayers —spiteful towards
Tabloid-branded *"spongers"* and *"benefit
Fraudsters"*— happily support and exhaustedly
Applaud for spending their money for them
And setting such 'graceful' examples to
The 'great unwashed' who underwrite them...

5.

A hollow *We* for *Me, Me, Me,* ta-ta Brian
Haw and back to Haw-Haw; O Boris 'by Jingo'
Albino Jolly John Bull and his blimpish
Minted imperials, along with Laughing
Farage and his purple-shirted apprentices,
His impostor pound sign *"People's Army"*
Of working-class turkeys marching to last Christmases;
Last-gasped gestures of togetherness
In lieu of less against ragged vestiges
Of corduroyed flares, Apache hair,
Transgressive vim —trimmed in Seventy-Nine,
Monetarily guillotined, forgetting better
Selves for brutish fruits, stamping on low-hanging
Brambles in the crush and grab for berries,
A gorging of juice-bruised chins... But long-
Shelved elements still in ferment can be
Smelted from melted entitlements to weld
A Peoples' Mandate, even up, pierce
Peasouper spins of internecine feuding,
Scrape salubrious asylum from valorised
Jerusalem's sieving visitations —given,
Vast numbers have been overwhelmed —
And over-weaned— through variolation
Of that acquisitive virus, *"Invisible Hand"*,
Avaricious vaccine proscriptive of giving,
Gold and contagious, more comte de Saint-Simon's
"Hand of Greed" inveigled into civic glove
To varnish scales with spit and vinegar... Rattled
By fiscal artilleries, it's difficult to see the cage
For the canary, dwarfed by wharfs, thwarting markets,
A Capital infatuated with its kleptocratic captors;
A bubo of disembodiment; a pustule
Burst by buss of pecking proctors —
Doughnut-London: prime sprawl of pawn-
Brokered democracy's Stockholm syndrome...

6.

It took brass orchestras of bombs and doodlebugs
To bruise a Bulldog Breed, jitterbugs
To shake off burdens' bombed-out homologies,
Jolt a mongrel pedigree to common purpose,
Build a Settlement of betterment from rubble
Of bombardment —sparks in Blitzed skies charted
Damascus paths to stars of slum-struck Attlees...
Now that Commonweal is clamped;
Cooperatives, the tenders of gentler nostalgias;
Prefabricated patching up of fractious classes,
Stripped with turpentine just thirty-three years after
Thatcher's velvet hatchet traumatised the plaster;
Feral elites unleashed through snipped *"red
Tapes"* —dead heat to *"repatriate powers"*,
Defenestrate the *"benefit cheat"* through
Smashed windows of the gutted Welfare State
(Bullingdon Blues *"Love the sound of breaking
Glass"*, demonstrably), to be put in public
Stocks and pelted with orange peels by
Red-top mobs; alpha-male amphibians
Rampant with ambitious bile more venomous
Than Margaret ever managed on her epic mile
From Grantham to Finchley and our Merry Hell...

7.

Now well-heeled prehensile heirs inherit
The title deeds, deliver her vicarious
Second reign of *"respectable greed"*
To table-thumping, cutlery-rattling, ra-ra-ra-ing
Riot Clubs, boisterously apotheosising
Their recently departed Carpocratian
Queen *"Maggie"* (who, after all, always assumed
The Royal *"We"*) into a marble hand-bagged
Gorgonic goddess of cupidity
To whom they spill postprandial tributes,
Proposing toasts to *"Thatcher Day"*;
And Cabinet architects are hatching plans
To reconstruct her cardboard cities

(Now retro design classics, endlessly recyclable):
Wrecking-balls poised to swing through urban
Reliquaries to yesterdays overspent;
Pens for spendthrifts sketched-in with pencils
Sharp as portcullises, compassing social
Sepulchres, sculpting out Vorticist chicken coops
For chronics, alcoholics, Lotto addicts,
Bottle tots weaned on Methadone's green milk —
Absinthe of abstinence from brown;
Crutched athletes primed for stomach-cramped
Paralympics, pole-vaulting on cold turkeys;
Malthusian landscaping, nettling ghettoes,
Pitched tents for stitched rents, newspaper
Tenements —already ring-fenced by unscrupulous
Slumlords of whom there's no shortage,
Damp-stained agents of Gentrification —
The piquancy of laminated pestilence:
A scent wafting in from the plastic fascist suites
Of ResPublica and Atlantic Bridge —
Rucksack chattels to swell the city's thirst
For absent tenants, Boris's newfangled breed
Of metropolitan ornamental hermits
Foraging in food banks, bargain bin-ends
Sponsored by Standard & Poor's downgradings;
Fly-tips hedged-in by inaccessible blackberries;
Municipal poverty porn for cupcake-licking,
Frappuccino-sipping pinstripes...

8.
At scum-caked Waterloo, silent rioters crouch,
Stiff as stalactites, coalblack as pit-stooped miners,
Or recline under branching arches dragging
Shadows back over vulnerable bodies,
Adjusting blankets of dark, interrupted
In public sleeps by torch-monocled Cyclops
Strobing to Tartarus stations, commuters
Hop-scotching mushroom-crops of homunculi
At this Pompeian flea-pit of swingeing bites...
St. Paul's silhouettes hover closer to scooping

Out the culprits into brutalising bright
Austerities that antler-pin their victims
Like startled stags in fog-lights; tip up sour
Milks of parasites; absentees spring-cleansing
Tenancies, clinking stucco empties;
Unsightlies culled to doughnut rings,
Sprinklings of *"Wrags"* triangulated
With gypsies, refugees, travellers, *"Chavs"*,
Squatters, *"Crusties"*, miracle *"shirkers"*,
Soup-scoured schizophrenics... Occupy
Springs scrupulous pincer-moves of its out-
Pincered movement, carves out Anarcho-
Syndicalist squats in vacated Swiss Holdings
Honeycombing Sun Street, Hackney's 'Bank
Of Ideas', amid bankrupted curries
Of brown congealed terraces... More crop up,
Prompt as pop-up shops; shadow welfare states
Catering for cuts outcasts —social care alfresco;
Soupçons of cooperatives, soiled coupons
Cropped to grow food parcels á la carte,
Tinned mush, Soylent escargot, truffles
Of the Trussell Trust —or *Biffa* bins of *Tesco*...

9.
Bailiff-raffled families, patched-up quandaries
Of choked community outreach, veterans
Un-invented in adventurists' spinached teeth,
Clapped by psychic Crimeas, bandaged, bluff-
Blindfolded, demobbed to Diaspora spilt
Onto uncompromising pavements, exposed
Like open wounds of post-traumatic stress,
Heroes of the violet hours, boot-bags for club-goers,
Stepped-over by ladies-of-the-lamplights' stilettos:
New tenants of toadstool streets keeping them
From doors of wolfing money-lenders,
Or penny-dreadful porches of debaucheries;
Tarpaulins sprouting from waterlogged funguses
Of rain-blotched eviction notices, damp
Trumpeting, umbrellas blossoming;

Propulsive buds of febrile February,
Tents beating trees into leaf; the Tent City
University dishing out bread and soup degrees,
Bucking trends of trebled fees... But pincers
Of the City's shadow landlords latch on to these
Anthracitic saints through grubbed legalities;
Chip their spark-carved visages from charred
Cathedral stone —lobster-potted desecrators;
Board them up in priest-holed hinterlands
Of lean-to Buy-To-Debts in burnt ashtray Prestons,
Red-rusted heartlands scored by sore-thumbed banners,
Cropped roses of derelict Labour Clubs'
Dialectical halls echoing full-circle
Back to draughty Baptist chapels;
Trumped Marxists at prayer, pews of humbled jumpers
Wheezing emphysema hymns, wasp-wing
Spectacles catching light or hunkering
In glooms behind snookered Trotskyite
Resigner lenses, Bolshevik bifocals
Blured by symbols of lugubrious God-Builders......

10.
Tip down South: pinstriped Houdinis slip
Regulations' thinning margins; no cooperatives
Tolerated to door-stop corporations,
Float their oscillating indexes, spike
Their computed temptations —Comptrollers
Are their keepers and protectors... But a sea-change
Is brewing, the ectopic pulse of fellowship
Is ripening through greening veins on wrists
Of wising children, the nation's blood is melting,
Congealing to sealing wax and anger
At bonuses for Robber Barons, bounces on
Unbalanced sheets of Baronet Chancellors,
Masters of Ballentrae-cum-Ballentaylor;
Shortfalls for renting serfs, squatters of burnt carpets,
Scorched Monopoly boards of sofa-surfers
And futon-flippers; an epidemic's welling,
The common mood darkening, outgrowing glooming

Inglenooks of malcontents at closing ranks
Clouding round opaque pools and pots,
Transparencies thick and slimed as mudbanks,
Capillaries siphoning patriotic profits offshore,
"Sweetheart deals" for kleptomaniac companies —
Sans sunset clauses— signed in disappearing inks
Of our Shadow Constitution underwritten
By synthetic cousins cushioning our deficits
Of spirit: a nation's toxic upholstering on
Antidepressants... No Tobin-robed Red Bishops,
Crimson Curates, spectral Thaxted Rectors,
Anti-capitalist Popes or other Spirituals outside
The Corporation gain the perforated ear
Of the premiere, nor curl the burning shell-likes
Of the eyeless, tongueless Speaker bent
Only to svelte templar presses on the metacarpals,
Masonic charades from the always-adjacent
Remembrancer perched up in his high-chair
Like a cryptic umpire —serpent-whisperer
In hollow-panelled Westminster, matchstick
Parliament a-crawl with woodlice rekindling
Damp tinder of flannelling Hansards, soap-
Scrubbed hands of Erskine May's Cunctators,
Green-book worshippers of occulting Portcullis
(*All of which is purely symbolic of course*)...

11.

Snowed-in by November winds, braced for iced
Decembers, the kettled encampment crouches,
So close to summoning the City to symbolic
Account, its stockbroker grubs, blights on
The alopecia-moulting scalp of the Big Smoke's
Webbing comb-over; cosmopolitan
Propinquities; contempt for its own captives —
The capped, cash-strapped, obscure,
Native victims of metropolitan corruptions:
Canning on such vast a scale breeds sardines
With sharp elbows, commuting salmon swimming
In i-pod solipsism, plugged into psychic

Dampers from sour-mouthed bespoken polluters,
Tube compartments crammed with misanthropic
Mycroft Holmeses thumbing through soggy
Metros in sweaty mobile Diogenes Club Class
Saunas... Gnats swarm at the Stock Exchange,
Glued to melting screens, partitioned off from
Public disenchantment with retrenching means,
Impoverishment of most under flimsy subterfuge
Of windfalls for the thrifty —snow flurries
For the trustified Few (reified fugues
For the Many); far-off as Norwegian outposts
In dandruff-and-talcum white-outs —
Black-ice wings beating at tundras of trade,
Bats' ears pricked by counterfeit frequencies,
Garlic-sharp amplifications of markets
Unreflective as vampiric mirrors; so close
Yet so far from driving stakes into ice-hearts
Of Paternoster's Nosferatus;
The Occupiers cordoned-off by gaffer-tape
From frost-bitten destinations: financiers
Scaled them first and milked them for profits...

12.
Still the chill tents pitch in for winter, fixed
As ice picks at the lips of triple precipices,
Shadowed by St. Paul's snow-capped penumbra,
Warped windshielder for a Vatican of Capital
That vacillate a nation over cashless crevasses;
Frosted protestors' stopping-point, a depot
Of lip-served supplies —*They* deemed the trespassers
Of public highways' oyster passes
Clammed to pearly impostors, Jack Cades,
Wat Tylers, Dick Turpins with vendettas;
They, the people, *hoi polloi*, the *demos*
Deemed the interlopers of democracy
For holding too many public demo-s;
No hindrance to parishioners trooping about
Their churchly business, skirting awkward
Reminders of their radical skyward tradition,

Gritted rudiments of The Message they've ever
Heard but never translated into good deeds,
Never merged into evergetism (Conservatives
And Sunday Christians elect Charity
To take care of their social consciences,
Invest individual salvations in grace-and-favour
Dividends) nor absorbed into their Nimbyish
Behaviours, avoiding pavement gazes
In case one is their Saviour's... Gone to graze
In wildernesses of long-doled decades since
His squatting refugee parents were turfed
Out from their cold unfurnished digs
In an empty townhouse basement, all shelters
Shut to them, written-off as *"intentionally*
Homeless", optionally rootless, electively
Exiled *"benefit tourists"*, after a botched
Abortion attempt broke rules as thin
As ditchwater in a dingy hostel toilet...

13.
Grown up now, that accidental Son,
Carpenter-by-trade, presently unemployed,
A prophet on the scrapheap, tagged a *"Wrag"*
And *"Scrounger", "Gypsy", "NEET", "Traveller",*
"Immigrant", "refugee", "insurgent", "anti-
Capitalist", "crypto-terrorist" and *"benefit cheat"*
For miracles undeclared (such as managing
To make a fortnight's giro stretch the whole
Two weeks) while claiming incapacity;
Stigmata of the claim stamp tattooed on his palms
Prayer-clasped up against Customer Compliance
In Booth Two Gethsemane, and an origami
Crown of thorns sculpted out of claim forms
And lacerating edges of tan paper envelopes...
He might be here amidst these lumpen Spartacuses,
Preaching hope and phoenixes, overturning
Money-changing counters of the markets
On His parabolic tongue before Pontius Pilates
Splash His feet in baptismal tasers

And crucify Him on two placards, after
Yellowed Judases betray Him and his kind
For thirty pieces of silver legislation
Glimpsed against the sulphur plush of a closing
Limousine door... Predestined to eviction
From ransomed shadows bruising in
The incubating Host, the Occupiers rupture through
To Paternoster Square, but not for long enough
To scour out its squirreling grey hideouts
With thought-thrown torchlights doused out as soon
As noticed; shuttered sunlight's no disinfectant,
Nor are tinted windows accountable to
Illuminations tilting on wilfully blind rooms...

14.
But through-drafts of unevictable ideas
Will blow the cobwebs from the catacombs,
Prise boulders to the bunged-up mouths
Of democratic tombs, empty the temples
Of their parasites, evict them from the breeding
Robber Baron ground they occupy deep inside
The rented British heart, its tissue purged
Of rouge and Raj, pyramidal chambers bled
Of empires but for blue hubristic lips
That still pimp imperially, trumpet antlered
Pelts striped with credit, mauled by mercantile,
Tigerish, hung up, stretched thin to spill
To maps of psychopathic pink, one last ditch
Adventurism, one last royal hunt of sunset
Enterprise before this island's capped to size,
And poverty's wolves come grovelling
In revenant forests felled to nourish fiscal cults;
Gaunt's green-vaunted realm razed to barrenness
And waste, Sargasso-grasping greed,
Leathery mint tentacles self-throttled
To scuffed fossils on broken shores of banshee-
Roared recoveries, too late for evacuees,
Washed-up seaweed refugees... Till all that's left
Standing: glazy trunks of lightning-struck trees,

Icons of deciduous-leafed *"selfies"*,
Gormless wooden Moai, shoulder-shorn torsos
Of one-eyed Dodo idols sprouting whittled crops
Atop a driftwood Katmandu of petrified
Bone-copse clawing at carcass-whistled
Rotted crates rattling with Neptune's retinues,
Wind-boomed busts sculpted in austerity's
Kraken-wake, staring out to choppy seas
Of baying waves and damply clapping slates...

RU-RI-TANNIA!
(After James Thomson's 'Rule, Britannia!')

Now Britain first, at Farage's command,
Choo-oo-oo-oose out from the a-a-a-zure mainland,
Choose, O choose ou-ou-ou-out from the a-zure flag
Twelve-star studded: tag Magna Carta, no more *"Jam
Tomorrow"* promises, but Marmalade today!
Angels in marble trilling *"Britain's Great Again"*:

*{Ru-ri-tannia!
How can ya' now complain?
Leavers ever, ever, ever shall re-main!}*

The mainland, no-o-o-o-ot so blest as we
With a Commonwealth (© the Queen):
Trade opportunities' bubble and squeak
In the wake of Empire's trumpeted poultry —
Brussels sprouts bureaucrats all mashed up,
Tipped out of the frying-pan into the camp fire,
And babes out with the bathwater,
No more Europe roped round our turkey neck,
We're taking our country back, *Cor blimey! By 'eck!*

*{Ru-ri-tannia!
How can ya' now complain?
We'll make the good old British banger grea-eat again!}*

While we get back our Liberty,
Our sausages and sovereignty,
Europe must in its turn, to ty-y-rants fall,
To a Bratwurst-supping Super-State
Of bureaucrats and social democrats —
A bunch of jumped-up Bonapartes,
Napoleons, Little Corporals, upstarts!
Well we may be a race of shopkeepers
But at least we'll be selling British produce
And once all the Polish hops-pickers

Are packed off back to Poland,
And the Latvians, Estonians and Lithuanians
Are uprooted from *Poundland*,
We'll put the Regis back in Bognor Riga,
We'll bid bon voyage to Johnny Foreigner,
To frogs' legs, bagels and Belgian lager,
We'll celebrate with cold pork pies and warm beer,
Morris Dancers on the village green, and good cheer!

{Ru-ri-tannia!
How can ya' now complain?
We'll make Great Britain Great all over again!}

We'll not miss the customs of the mainland,
We'll not miss their goulash of languages,
Newcomers from the Commonwealth will understand
Our lingo well enough to take down our orders,
We're going back to Tory-blue passports
(Even though they were actually black in the past!),
We're taking back control of our borders,
In part, by trying to plant one in France —
No we'll certainly not miss the mainland
Once we kick ourselves off from French shores,
Cast ourselves adrift —that is, liberate ourselves;
No more a mere vassal state of the Continent,
But an offshore fantasy island circus tent!
With any luck we'll drift across the Atlantic
And latch ourselves onto America's rump,
We're packing our trunk with a *trumpety-trump*
Trump-trump-trump...

{Ru-ri-tannia!
What if we now complain?
Once the immigrants are gone who do we blame?}

Sticking Agincourt salutes up at Europe,
And no matter what the Continentals throw at us
We'll rise above it, rise still more maje-e-estic,
More dre-e-e-eadful from each foreign stroke,
More dreadful, dreadful from each foreign stroke,
Bang go our employment and human rights,
But we'll shout *Hoorah! Hoorah!* for each stroke
Of the licking cat o' nine tails with which we
Thrash our national back rapturously —
Each poke of the Mote in the Beam-end serves
But to further ro-o-o-ot thy Tory oak...

{Ru-ri-tannia!
Will UKIP up its game?
Once we've got our country back can we give it away?}

Here's to pomp and ceremony in our tin-pot kingdom,
To unreconstructed monarchy,
Bunting and punting and pageantry
In this Land of Anthony Hope's old story,
The Prisoner of Zenda: yes, ironically
Our country will more resemble Ruritania,
That small Germanic realm set in a permanent
Nineteenth century —Continental Uchronia;
Or the even more backward aspic-
Pickled Duchy of Grand Fenwick
In Leonard Wibberley's *The Mouse That Roared*
(Although we're more a Squeaking Lion
When it comes to any influence abroad) —
We might lose our rainbows but we'll keep our unicorns!
O back to old boys, yobs, snobs, noblesse oblige,
Sir Nigel, Boris Greenback, and Baron Rees Mogg,
John Bull, Blimp, Bagpuss and Noggin the Nogg,
Double barrel-land, and bally Baden-Powell,
Rivers of blood, Toby jugs, Patron Saint Enoch (Powell),
Let the wind rush through our ivory sails,
We'll rule the waves again, well, at least as far as Wales!

{Ru-ri-tannia!
Our Pe-di-gree Re-gained:
(In no par-tic-u-lar order:) Pict-
Celt-Gael-Saxon-Norman-Dane...

Ru-ri-tannia!
U-ni-ted once a-gain
Under mongrel flags a-a-nd so many damn names...}

Drain the Swamp

Now white supremacists doing Nazi-style salutes
To Donald Trump, *sieg heil*-ing in Washington DC
Openly for all to see on mobile phone footage —
Not blue collars or rust-belt rednecks but dapper
Men in sharp suits, *Hugo Boss* wardrobed
Businessmen —self-made plutocratic products
Of the globalization of capitalism
That they promise to stamp out from the nation
On behalf of those who feel left behind,
Whom *they* left behind to fill up their carpet-
Bags to spilling point, now they'll find a place
For them, the putupon lumpenproletariat
Of America, simply by dumping on numberless
Of their own compatriots: immigrants, foreigners,
Homosexuals, people of colour, Mexicans,
Blacks, Moslems, Native Americans, and
In their place come new opportunities for
Blue collars and red necks of the dispossessed
Rust-belts and dustbowls who'll dust off
The cobwebs of those pointy white hoods,
While the white supremacists rampantly
Promote their race of Wasps and Aryan
Evangelicals in a bid to *"make America
Great again"* —but what that means depends
On how many memes make five and on what
Humpty Dumpty Trump says and whatever it means —
All America waits to see if he'll drain
That swamp, build that wall, burn that bridge,
Or make a mountain out of a hill of beans...

The Pigeon Spikes

Pigeons perch on the scrawny shoulders
And bony elbows of the Big Issue vendor
Who pitches outside the supermarket
Near where unsponsored rough sleepers
Mutely appeal with cupped hands or empty
Cardboard *Costa Coffee* cups for pennies
In spite of Public Space Protection Orders,
And fly defiantly in the face of *"defensive
Architecture"*: buildings fortified
With metal studs cemented like gummed
Teeth to deter human vertebrae, while
Bus stops are benchless but for narrow
Sloping plastic bum-perches, and park
Benches are newly segmented by iron
Arm-rests to guard against vagrants
Lying down to get some shuteye...

The vendor thinks, if only he could pull in
As many punters as pigeons that settle on
The spindly perches of his shoulders;
If only his palms filled up with pound coins
As much as with crumbs for pecking beaks
Of cooing columbiformes; but then
This is his special gift from the grit of circumstance:
To be a living statue for pigeons to perch on...

But it can only be a matter of time until
This curious purpose turns metamorphosis:
For rumours moot the homeless are now
Little more than anthropomorphised pigeons,
Discouraged from roosting at night in sheltered
Entranceways or porches to posh apartments
By the sprouting of small metal spikes,
Blunt-tipped but thoroughly uncomfortable,
Knobbly to the back if one was to sprawl
Upon them for an acupunctural nap,

Spine-nudging studs, beds of blunt nails,
The most literal of blunt instruments,
Toothed oysters, foldout lilo iron maidens —
(Though better by far than being tipped out
Into rubbish crunchers from *Biffa* bins);
Similar to those spikes put on tops of railings
To send out clear messages to winging pigeons
Not to perch there on pain of being impaled —
Not so much a *'hand up'* as a *spike up*
That place where the sun don't shine! Look,
People: *pigeon spikes to repel rough sleepers!*
Not so much as a coo from the popular press —
Just ricocheting *"Scrounger"* quips from the *Express*...

So man and pigeon cooperate, homeless
Homo sapien and proscribed columbiforme
Pitch in together, sculpt out a strange
Familiar solidarity: human head
And shoulders for perches, mangy pigeon
Plumage for feathered umbrellas... (*Now only*
Shadows get heads down under porches)...

Kipling Buildings

If you can keep your head when all about you
Are spy cameras, a deliberate delay
Of the appointment time in an attempt
To break your spirit, a protracted wait
In a claustrophobic, clinical-looking room,
A neutrally decorated purgatory
Silent except for the rumbling water cooler,
Being observed by unseen deciders
Prolonging your agony in a pot-plant garden...

If you can keep your head during a gruelling
Interrogation at Independent Assessment
Services (formerly Atos Solutions),
Being asked trick questions, being observed,
Recorded, monitored, not listened to,
Only heard, not being respected or
Empathised with, but being judged
In an unacknowledged kangaroo court
Of icy stares and sporadic mouse-clicks
For each of the ticks in the boxes on
The assessor's screen turned away from you
So you can't see —while being observed
Just as a troubled adolescent by
A cryptic psychiatrist's invisible observers
Behind two-way glass; these desk-perched
Harpies who prey on the sick and disabled
For sport, will pick off your weak points
And press all your buttons to get the most
Pool-muddying responses to cloud your claim...

If you can keep your PIP when all about you
Are losing theirs, it'll only be a pyrrhic
Victory, a temporary reprieve, just putting off
The inevitable sting of a future trap-sprung
Reassessment, opportunity for symptom-
Tampering and a spot of goalpost-changing
To ensure next time you're lower scoring...

If you can keep your nerve at Independent
Assessment Services nestled deep
In the grey, mauve and periwinkle plush
Of Kipling Buildings poorly disguised
As a clinic but whose commercial shape
And façade indicate that a bank once
Operated there, on the nondescript corner
Of a pigeon-grey street in an unexplored
Part of Portsmouth, then you will be damned,
My son, damned with a disability,
But worse, an invisible one, and the points
You'll score will be in binary numbers —
The price for their bounties, their thirty pieces...

Rudyard Digs
after Kipling

There's a special place in 'ell reserved for landlords —
A rabbit hutch (h'advertised: 'one bedroom flat')
In which they has to cram n' stew together
In a tiny space partitioned-up to pat:
A kitchen, living room and makeshift diner
H'an insultin' size to even sty-cramped pigs;
Wiva' a fold-out bed what pokes you wiv' a shiner
If you tries to fold it out in these grim digs...

There's a special place in 'ell reserved for landlords —
Its walls all black and blue with damp n' mould
N' fungus growing out like little trumpets
That if kept unchecked can get a stranglehold —
N' if that ain't punishment enough, there's rent
They has to cough up every month on time
What is priced inversely to their cranky slum-hass':
Something like a grand a head —a damp-light crime...

N' before they're each permitted to move in
A thasand of 'em tinned in sardine-tight
(They has to negotiate h'an open oven
To get their bleedin' 'eads down of a night),
They must first fork out for h'an 'olding deposit,
A first month's rent 'n' same plus more besides
Before they gain the privilege of shelter
N' counts their blessings while flames lick their 'ides...

The Bricks of Henrietta Street

Comrades don't despair in this red wilderness
For it's red for a reason, red stains permanently
As blood, blood of bold ideas congealing,
And this blood will solidify into earthy red,
Terracotta-red of the bricks of Henrietta Street,
Brick-red, brick-orange, burnt orange, red
Orange, blood orange, browning orange,
And stiffen into woven cloth covers that will
Bind boundless books in pockmarked gourds,
Leathery orange peels, hundreds on hundreds
Of truth-telling titles, social documents,
Commentaries, reportage perfect-bound
In blood-grubby bandages, poultices
Of polemic, exposés of contemporary
Poverties and injustices that red-tops portray
As taboo, the sin not of unemployment
But of simply being unemployed, in spite
Of capitalism's dependency on a surplus
Unemployed population to keep wages down
For those in employment, and tie their hands,
No room for negotiations when threatened
With umpteen replacements from an ever-
Replenishing pool of cheap labour —more
And more employers boycotting unions...

After eight years under austerity tsars,
Now, at last, in the Noughteens —retro-twinned
With the Nineteen Thirties— print-antidotes
To right-wing hegemonies are returning,
The writing of a new generation germinating
Red energies charging blood in biros and red
Ink in veins: the legendary Left Book Club
Is winging its way back onto shelves of red
Believers everywhere, subscribers to a new
Breed of red belles-lettres ringing red bells
Of rebellion, counter-narratives to tattered

Austerity mantras... Come, comrades,
Fill your shelves with news from nowhere
Travelling everywhere, social documents
Ricocheting round lean-tos, slums, bedsits,
Garrets, studios, grottos and doughnut-ghettos;
Pluto is publishing what promise to be
Social scriptures of our times, printed witness,
Once the special preserve of a certain type
Of bespectacled sophisticate, culture-steeped
Contradiction, most notably one Victor
Gollancz, Fabian publisher and anti-fascist
Activist, Guild socialist and entrepreneur,
Rabbi's son and Christian, Gentile and Jew,
Visionary of Maida Vale, along with fellow
Left-wing luminaries, Stafford Cripps,
Harold Laski, John Strachey, back in the austere
Thirties, which lit up every left-leaning
Library in Britain with volumes uniformed
In fervid liveries, singed orange paperbacks,
Red hardbacks, clothbound bricks of bristling
Literature of social witness —titles printed
Horizontally across the tops of their spines
And in plain bold capitals upon their covers
Blank but for the imprint's art deco logo,
And blazoned along the foot of each book,
The legend: NOT FOR SALE TO THE PUBLIC —
Ironic for such an iconic socialistic
Enterprise so all-encompassing— but LBC
Books were only purchasable by subscription,
And circulated exclusively among a progressive-
Minded membership, titles that thundered,
Demanded to be read, not slipped off the shelf
So much as slipped on as philanthropic aprons:
The Problem of the Distressed Areas;
Fallen Bastions; Our Threatened Values;
Can Capitalism Last?; The Acquisitive
Society; Savage Civilisation; A Catholic
In Republican Spain; A Short History
Of Unemployment; Penn'orth of Chips;

These Poor Hands; The Town that was Murdered;
The Road to Wigan Pier; Barbarians
At the Gate; Rosa Luxembourg; The Betrayal
Of the Left; The Left Song Book; Left Wing
Democracy in the English Civil War;
Hammer or Anvil; In Darkest Hungary;
History has Tongues; Walls have Mouths;
Smouldering Freedom; The Darker the Night,
The Brighter the Stars; Spanish Testament;
Under the Axe of Fascism; Kaffirs are
Lively; Towards the Christian Revolution;
Rats!; Money; So Many Hungers; Waiting
For Lefty; Women Must Choose; The Scum
Of the Earth; Scorched Earth etcetera —so
Many striking titles with which to conjure
By assorted writers and thinkers of the Left:
Wilfred Wolfendale, Ella Lingens-Reiner,
André Malraux, Katharine Burdekin,
Clement Attlee, G. D. H. Cole, Edgar Snow,
Oliver Walker, Amber Blanco White,
Simon Haxey, Palme Dutt, J.B.S Haldane,
Nye Bevan, George Orwell, Arthur Koestler,
Leonard Woolf, David W. Petegorsky,
Clifford Odets, "Red" Ellen Wilkinson,
Alan Bush, Randall Swingler, Léon Blum,
R. H. Tawney, Gaetano Salvemini, Alan Beck,
Wilfred Macartney, Wal Hannington et al,
And spawned national LBC reading groups
Harnessing the knowledge-hungry eagerness
Of working-class autodidacts, the print
Turned into a movement... And now, once
More, time for those of social conscience
To compose more polemics on the symptoms
And pathologies of a decaying society
Which once more dumps on its poor, dispossessed,
Unemployed, homeless, incapacitated,
In this dawn of the welfare state's dismantling,
Of social cleansing flimsily disguised as
"Gentrification" in new eugenics lexicon...

Well, let's gentrify the coarse-grained elephantine
Hide of the thick, rough, rigid twenty-first
Century English skin, smooth out those wrinkles
With a bit of common sense and compassion,
With these paper salves of philanthropic prose,
Egalitarian writing, no mere cosmetics,
But more authentic cures to the callousness
Of our Thatcheritic culture, our wintry,
Treeless intellectual climate of counterfeit
Reality TV, property-worship, empty
Consumerism, conspicuous consumption,
Precariousness, scroungermongering —
Let's tell it like it is outside the tinted
Limousines and penthouse suites of MPs,
The privet hedges and private drives, let's
Throw each clothbound brick of compassionate
Polemic through portcullised windows...

Now once more books need to be mobilised
Against the oncoming monsoon of moral
Panic and scapegoating, in the face of a new
Gentrified fascism, a bespoke chauvinism,
Fitted out in chalk-striped suits with broad
Sharp lapels of dapper Rees-Moggs and flush
Farages and their xenophobic apostles
Poisoning the well of tolerant discourse
And spreading ugly rumours around immigrants
And refugees now Brexit has given tacit
Licence to a 'fascism of the shires' to surface
Through the rhetoric of Tories and Ukippers,
And the random acts of discrimination
And violence almost normalised now
In the mainstream through galumphing Trump
The blond toupee-topped populist strong man
Of America, and, on the Continent from
Which this shabby island is steadily cutting
Itself adrift, Marine le Penn's Front Nationale,
Geert Wilders' Dutch Freedom Party,
Hungary's Jobbik, Greece's Golden Dawn,

Italy's Five Star Movement, the Sweden
Democrats, and the Tommy Robinson-
Supporting stompers at home (and abroad),
All the rest of uncompromising patriotic
Factions, protectionists, nationalists, fascists,
And their hack apparatchiks in the cherry-
Picking red top press who weaponise
Polemical prose into rifle-cocking rhetoric,
Unfortunately, *FOR* SALE TO THE PUBLIC...

But those old LBC tomes still pack a punch,
Are ever-relevant as roseate revenants
On shelves of today's second-hand charity
Bookshops, spines warped, distressed, but still
Standing out in their blazing red, scarlet,
Crimson, tomato, orange, foxed and tanned
Pages musty with Thirties and Forties'
Tobacco-scent —our Uchronian chronicles...

Either those red and orange bricks were made to build things
Or be thrown through windows of established buildings —
But those paper bricks built bridges across class divides,
So be it for their belated return, books are being mobilised...

Zaghareet

A shaven-headed brick-orange man
Barges past a woman in a brown hijab
Outside *Sainsbury's*, and noticeably
Abjures an apology —but in any case
A *"Sorry"* in Bognorese sounds more
Like a verbal blow: a stroppy *"So-roi"*;
As he bursts out with shopping bags
Bulging from his fists like boxing gloves
Back onto the unlistening street,
The sliding doors closing behind him
Emit a high-pitched ululation
Like a greeting chorus of Arab women—
A half-strangled *zaghareet*...

Shabby Gentile

Shabby Gentile believes in bricks and mortar,
In football, pubs and the great British banger,
He's a bluebottle nose and a cauliflower ear,
Shaved head shaped like a potato, a bruiser,
Brain clenched in a fist —a neighbour
Who'll shop you to jobcentreplus if he spies
Telltale tan envelopes in your recycling,
Confirming suspicions you're not declaring
Your curtains shut during the day, white lies,
Topping up below-inflation benefits
With a spot of cash-in-hand moonlighting
In the small zero hours' whirligigging...

Shabby Gentile thinks benefits are too generous,
Agrees, in this regard, with the *Daily Express*,
The Sun, Daily Mail, News of the World (God rest
Its bacon roll —if not Full English breakfast) —
The red tops that spoon-feed him his opinions;
Newspaper ink fumes are his daily poisons...

Shabby Gentile believes in honest hard work,
Has nothing but knuckles for those who shirk,
But admires and aspires to the self-made man
Who's helped himself up with invisible hand
Then kicked away the ladder —legerdemain:
Pulling rabbits of profits out of upturned hats
Of others' robbed labour for his ill-gotten gain...

Shabby Gentile believes in British jobs
For British workers, hoists the St. George cross
On a flagpole outside his semi-detached,
Its mortgage paid off by skint tenants' rents,
Shortfalls stumped up with housing benefits
For his mould-infested Buy-to-Let flats:
No smokers, no DSS, no dogs, no cats —
Once bills are paid it's a trip to the foodbanks...

Shabby Gentile voted Brexit but has
No intention of staying, like the other ex-pats,
Off to brown off in his Union Jack
Boxer shorts once he's got his country back —
Only grey skies spike his patriotism
Otherwise he'd have spent his retirement
In his native privets, loves his country,
Thoughts of *'long shadows over county grounds,*
Warm beer, invincible green suburbs, dog
*Lovers and pools fillers'** get his bottom lip
Wobbling, eyes misting to nostalgic fog,
But he can't stand the weather, wants a tan,
Not a natural one, that's too Taliban,
Something slapped on in a tanning salon
Along the fault-lines of Trump's Orangutan,
Though more likely he'll turn pink as the map
Of the old British Empire; he's patriotic
But can't pinpoint any actual reason for it:
His allegiances are visceral, primitive, tribal,
Expressed in cheap flags and facepaint at football...

Shabby Gentile has his head shaved weekly
To keep it cropped on top and stubbly
Round the back and sides, like a new recruit,
Or a Blackshirt to put it more bluntly,
And some of his views on refugees,
Roma and immigrants aren't so far removed...
Though he's only Ukip/ EDL/ Britain First
On a Saturday night when he's slaking his thirst —
All foreigners are infidels, all Muslims are Isis;
Lock up your passports when he's out on the piss!

Shabby Gentile is allergic to change,
The mere word 'progressive' brings him out in a mange;
He's tried to kick the fags but just can't get on
With vaping —he needs a light to lighten
Up the tip and singe it to a dog end...

Shabby Gentile is eternally grateful
To the Iron Lady, *Gord rest 'er soul*;
Good old Maggie brought the blue collar
Up some rungs on the property ladder
Even if she destroyed manufacturing and coal
And put 3 million or more on the dole
And turned Care in the Community
Into mass homelessness and Cardboard City —
She turned Shabby Gentile from an anxious corporal
Hungry for knowledge to a tabloid troll
Greedy for ignorance, prejudice and vitriol,
Hostile to study, militantly anti-cultural;
The smokeless local pub, his place of worship,
His epistolary, a scribbled *Ladbrokes* tip...

Blue collar, white collar, white van man,
All variables of Shabby Gentile and
If there's one thing they all believe in it ain't
The brotherhood of man but a new lick of paint,
Some vague Shangri-La in a newfangled car
Or a retail park's shop-potting utopia —
Shabby Gentiles are defined by their urge
To try and move over the shivering verge
Of privet-hedged bets to better themselves
Not in terms of books but in terms of shelves —
They're not concerned with what ifs but what is-es,
In getting things done *rand the hass*, you might
Term them *"jam tomorrow"* Benthamites,
They've no time for dreams or idealisms,
Only for eel pies and empiricisms,
Dropping their aitches and rhyming their slang,
Dupes of employment, no more red brethren,
They don't know their Robert Tressell but do
Know their trestle tables —precious few
Jack Londons among them, nor Frank Owens,
Lord Jims, Martin Edens or Obscure Judes...

Shabby Gentile instinctively envies
Those just above him, instinctively sneers
At those just beneath —a bit of a Humpty-
Numpty but without the riddles, just smutty
Jokes, wolfwhistles, double entendres
(Excuse his French) blue language for red ears,
An amateur stand-up comic in the old
Sweary and smoky working men's club mould;
Pronouncing things properly isn't his style:
Gabbles the name of his tribe: *Shabbigentile*...
Shabby Gentile keeps his inarticulate
Anti-Semitism under his belt but hate
Is the petrol that runs his engine —hate
Against anyone to whom he can't relate,
Anyone who doesn't fit his cramped template
Of employment, property, consumerist taste;
Shabby Gentile's a bottled-up Genie
Of judgemental memes, a mind-vigilante,
And he has access to an Aladdin's Cave
Of more acceptable prejudices against
The poor, unemployed, disabled, immigrants,
Refugees, gypsies, Roma, single mothers,
Hobos, bohos, homos, squatters, travellers,
Rough sleepers, soft dreamers, students, druggies,
Hasn't any time for the underclass or Chav,
Navigates his hates like a ranting Sat Nav...

Shabby Gentile's your jingoistic Cabbie,
Your xenophobic plumber, your cursing brickie,
Your intransigent Bluetoothed bailiff, or bouncer,
Your obdurate jobsworth at the call centre,
But he can also be your tight-fisted landlord,
Your stroppy debt-collector promoted to clipboard,
Your bespoke inspector of benefit fraud...

Just to think that not so long ago as
The Nineteen Seventies Shabby Gentile was
Union rep, shop steward, shipbuilder, miner,
And in most respects a paid-up Labour member;
But Thatcher's prime accomplishment, her coup
Was to turn the Red Gentile Shabby and Blue;
He's still a shopkeeper in many respects:
But the shop is now his home, heaped up
With products he's hypnotised to purchase
In spite of their built-in obsolescence,
Rather like pink-striped Bagpuss, his bay
Window doubles up as a shop display...

Shabby Gentile believes the only way to gauge
Someone's moral worth is if they earn a wage,
Believes as long as you have a job
You're a moral paragon, even if a yob
In private, full of spite and resentment
Towards claimants of state entitlement;
Believes true democracy is rule by the mob,
Shows open contempt for the cosmopolitan,
Distrusts intellectuals, snubs bohemians,
Shabby chic cliques and trustafarians
(Who sniff at his kind as oafs, vulgarians,
Parvenus, arrivistes, ogres, what-have-yous),
His story steeped in proud philistinism
Turned to an art form, a supreme mission,
Ignorance is bliss, won't mess with the brand,
Peter Bazalgette is his Chateaubriand,
And, like Paul Dacre and his Scabrous Brand,
Demonises what he doesn't understand...

Shabby Gentile's allegiance to regina
Is the strangest thing in a stranger arena,
Against his own interests he's happy to pay
Taxes for the upkeep of empty palaces,
Supporting a superrich family
As it reproduces its dependency
On cash-strapped taxpayers it deigns to call

Its 'subjects' —while he resents every penny
Spent on benefits for the unemployed,
Sick, disabled, single mothers especially;
Shabby Gentile's a tangle of allegiances
And antagonisms, spite and prejudices;
Applauds his captors and claps his exploiters,
Is happily played for red-top Tory sport,
A baggy trousered misanthropist, self-taught
Pugilist, thuggish upgrade of *Ingerland*'s
Ear-ringed and tattooed new middling sort...

Shabby Gentile's just doing his job —
Shabby Gentile's *Not being funny, but...*
He has an opinion on how people should be:
Work, consume, own their own property,
And other peoples', buy up the empties,
Do them up, rent them out or sell them on —
There's nothing one can't make a profit from —
Anyone who deviates from this type of lifestyle
Is suspect in the eyes of Shabby Gentile...

Shabby Gentile brings home the bacon
For his pigs in blankets —he's the gammon,
Something in his gut roots for Tommy Robinson
(Though less so for Stephen Yaxley-Lennon)...

From Pearly King to pie-crust Yorkshireman,
See all, hear all, say nowt, keep schtum
When it comes to homegrown discrimination
On the basis of race, faith or pheromone,
From matt-coated troll to gloss-daubed gnome
Shabby Gentile flies the ensign at home,
His brick castle turreted with rolled-up *Sun*s,
Feels besieged by foreigners who speak in Tongues,
Baa-barbarians banging at the angry gates
Of Saturday stadiums, Brobdingnagian
Games played against ghosts and scapegoats
And whoever else fills the changing goalposts,
Shabby Gentile likes to keep a tidy garden,
Razor-short lawn, grass attitudes harden...

Shabby Gentile's just doing his job,
Shabby Gentile hopscotches the cross,
Sticking in thorns, driving in nails,
Every day delivers routine betrayals,
But it's himself he betrays most of all;
More than his job's worth to question his boss
(That shadowy figure who pulls his strings);
No angel in marble, more a thug in gloss,
The devil's in the detail of bluntest sculpting,
He's an incubus of emotional blunting...
Shabby Gentile has enough on his plate
Without washing other people's dishes,
He's no time for grassers or Judases,
And washes his hands of Pontius Pilates...

Shabby Gentile's just doing his job —
Shabby Gentile's *Not being funny, but...*

62

The Problem with Jeremy
(or, Jeremy Mixes with the Wrong Kind of Jews)

We must be accountable for company we choose:
Jeremy Corbyn mixes with the wrong kind of Jews...

Jeremy has the most questionable views,
Jeremy addresses unfashionable issues
(At least not the kind that will make the news),
Jeremy mixes with the wrong kind of Jews...

Jeremy fraternizes with militants,
Leftists, extremists, all the worst elements,
Brings the Labour Party into disrepute
By bringing it back to its grassroots,
Gleaning more working-class, younger recruits
(And by wearing rather shabby flannel suits)...

Jeremy prefers not wearing a tie,
Jeremy's an MP who simply won't lie,
Jeremy calls out Israel when its missiles
Target unarmed Palestinian juveniles —
Jeremy is an unapologetic Gentile...

Jeremy's economy would choke green shoots,
Drive business away, stifle innovation,
Trample enterprise under nationalisation;
Jeremy grows his own vegetables and fruits
On his common allotment in Islington —
Quite the modern day Winstanley totem,
Figurehead of Diggerish cult Momentum...

Jeremy's an enemy of the nation:
He won't promise to bring about its destruction
By pressing the big red nuclear button
Thus setting in motion a chain reaction
Of atomic catastrophe and radiation —
He's most unclear about our incineration...

Jeremy's completely unpatriotic,
Tieless at the cenotaph, just as quixotic
As Michael Foot was in his donkey jacket—
Socialism on the back of a fag packet...

Jeremy's wardrobe is casual and beige,
He likes to wear track suits befitting his age;
A bearded sandal-wearer —he's no early bird,
'Jeremy's not good in the mornings', we've heard...

Jeremy champions the poor and oppressed,
The outcast, marginalised, dispossessed,
Refugees, immigrants, unemployed, homeless,
In complete contempt of public opinion/
The poisonous spoon of the red top press...

Jeremy's the unelectable they keep electing,
Jeremy has the Establishment trembling,
Jeremy's too nice to call out the Kremlin,
Jeremy's an enemy of democracy,
Jeremy won't kneel to the monarchy,
Jeremy's a gnome, a goblin, a gremlin,
Jeremy's a troll calling Billy Goats' bluff,
Jeremy's a Jeremiah at the last gasp of capitalism,
Jeremy's just full of old Red Flag guff,
Jeremy has an unstatesmanlike style,
Jeremy knows his resistance is futile,
Jeremy's simply the wrong kind of Gentile,
Jeremy's a friend of Hezbollah and Hamas,
Jeremy celebrated Seder with Jewdas,
Jeremy's 'for the many, not the Jew',
Jeremy puts our feet in other peoples' shoes,
Jeremy's an atheist with Christian views,
Jeremy mixes with the wrong kind of Jews...
Jeremy mixes with the wrong kind of Jews...
Jeremy mixes with the wrong kind of Jews...

"St. Jude" & the Welfare Jew

One might well ask why are there any Jews in the world order? That would be exactly like asking why are there potato bugs? Nature is dominated by the law of struggle. There will always be parasites...

—Joseph Goebbels circa 1933

I am a fan of benefit vouchers... for those who are drug users or alcoholics, those who have mental illness and those who have previously committed benefit fraud. ...Neither should the state fund uncontrolled childbirth. ...When the state funds feckless families there is no limit to the children they can have... Child benefit should be restricted to three children. A larger family is a lifestyle choice. ...If you start to withdraw benefits... then that is a first step to weaning them off the taxpayer. ...You cannot imagine many deadbeat parents using benefits to buy a book to help their children read before they start school. ...Until it is made worthwhile for everyone to work...there will be more parasites...

—Janice Atkinson, the *Daily Express*, 8 March 2013

1.
Newspapers make up news, red tops interpolate
Our everyday reality and pummel and crumple
Its foldable edges to accommodate
Camouflaged agendas of private investors'
Vested interests —the press keeps us
In perpetual present*ness* as a surplus
Populace of shopaholic schizophrenics;
Advertising manufactures actuality —
Though we're told we can choose whichever version
Of reality we wish, they're only microscopic
Scalloped replicas from the same root-mould,
Carbon copies you couldn't slip a cig-paper between,
Scaling ever-regressing variegations of right-wing,
Representing a *"free press"* only in the sense
It's *"free"* for those who are in ownership,
But not for its great unwashed readerships
For whom it's a warm and pulpy slip-on prison
(There must be more to 'democracy' than simply
Opting for others to form our opinions...?)...

2.

Our daily agendas are set not by parties
But red-top parrots of blue torch opinions
Igniting blue-touch tabloids, cropped topics,
Pre-packaged antagonisms, analgesic
Propagandas, austerity narratives (mystified
"Deficits" spouted by parliamentary
Performing monkeys to the organ-ground
Groove of the Troika and Markets), and spot-
The-*"sponger"* splashes snatching our attentions
From hectoring newsstands, tall tales
Of *"benefit cheats"*, *"handout"* Trolls,
"Scrounger" Ogres, Giro-ghouls and other
Struggling grotesques —out of frothing mouths
Of rabid Malthusians and poison pen Mendelists,
Scissor-tongued columnists pitching stereotypes,
Hyperbolic constructs for public spite,
Populist polemic couched in eugenics-
Inflected lexicon —*"feckless"*, *"parasites"*,
"Malingerers", *"workshy"* etcetera— punting
Out straw-boater hate with straw man arguments
And Oxbridge-borne opprobrium channelled
By the A.N. Wilson/ Janice Atkinson
Neo-Goebbels Brigade castigating an
Aktion Arbeitsscheu ("Work-shy") Reich
Of their own rhetorical making:
The common mythology of the *"Scrounger"*
('Scroungerology') of Jungian shadow-
Projection that pours out our problems
Into sample shampoos of self-escaping
Prejudices, malicious lotions, agents
Of social-engineering, unguents of *'nudging'*,
Viral salves that sublimate private vices
Into public taboos, scapegoat-prescriptions,
Special potions of point-score systems
And doctored descriptors sprouting phantom limbs
For amputees, sponsored by Atos Solutions/
Capita Spas/ Maximus Miracle Cures,
Persecutory tonics bottled in novelty

Folk-devil vessels, anthropomorphic moulds
Of near-tangible undesirables drip-fed
With coupons, penalties, sanctions and gas-tap
Stigmas hissing imperceptibly;
The unemployed, punch-bags for moral panics,
Public pin-cushions for spivs of voodoo doles...

3.
Contrapuntal to this Benefits Diaspora,
The papers whipped up another phantom storm
In October Twenty-Thirteen, setting
Itchy teeth on edge for the morning thunder
After the night before 28th of the month:
Projections of trees torn out from their roots —
Each yew-stump, a rotten tooth; pugilist gusts
And phalange-grappling gales; muscular
Hurricanes wrenching out power-lines across
The exposed Home Counties —and a battering
Of coastal chalk fortresses grinding away
In blustery fits of Bruxism, like crumbling
Symplegades —another whirlwind *a la*
Nineteen Eighty-Seven... only, it barely
Happened, although many swear that it did,
And there's the footage to pay media-edited
Testament to it; prompt reports to persist
With the fantasy that there was a storm,
According to data and statistics of casualties
To back it up, and multiple witnesses —
So much meteorological agitprop; weather
Forecasters —as with ratings agencies pace
Standard & Poor's and Moody's, and pin-
Striped pundits in thick-rimmed designer
Glasses —can't *all* be wrong... *Can they?*
Small matter either way: our inscrutable
British mentality opts by default to believe
The very worst without evidence, the more
Counterintuitive the more incontrovertible,
As if wilfully submitting to an insubstantial
'Faith' —but 'faith' in what? Fatalism...?

4.

Britons automatically opt not for miracles
But curses; pestilences complement
The pessimistic national character —in this case,
A blast of bad weather, a wind-tossed spectacle;
We being a temperamental people,
Elementally mercurial for our capricious
Island climate of soughing grey skies,
Inveterately overcast, through which we vent
Our blustery frustrations and gusts of disgust—
We vote with our weathervanes,
Pointing every which way the wind's choppy
Rhetoric throws us; we're only political
Within the scope of clouded forecasts,
Focuses for our disenfranchised furies,
Vicarious spleen-vents on cumulus prospects,
Storm clouds, high winds, historically low turnouts;
So disposed to poor moods, so gloomily
Accustomed to disappointment, to not
Expecting any good to come from anything
In this dry-rotting, grotty little tin-pot kingdom,
Where only prices and apathies rise up
With the damp; so sanitised to comfortable
Glumness in our bloated sofas; a psychical
Damp-proofing to preclude the creeping mould
Of disgruntlement and protect against
Sudden ruptures of despair that we've accepted
We're simply a land of soap and mostly Tory:
Attitudinally rigid, heart-hardened, hope-
Constipated, or suitably embittered by
Establishment betrayals, those that have happened
And those that are forecast to happen in the Braille-
Embossed brochures of unforeseeable futures,
That we think it better to presume the worst
Of ourselves and others (especially those
Who ask for something, whether asylum,
Sanctuary or state assistance e.g. claimants,
Immigrants and foreigners —all 'benefit tourists',
'Malingerers' and 'shirkers' of a kind, milking

Our human kindness), presume headline-grabbing
Guilt before un-newsworthy innocence;
Assume the Lamb once rumoured to have come
To our green resentful land was just a wet-
Footed refugee from Jerusalem seeking
Our *"soft-touch"* asylum, an empty promise —
Or purse— a wolf in scapegoat's clothing —
A hope-fleecing phantom, an impostor Peter Pan...

5.
What more appropriate sobriquet to bestow
On that phantom storm than *"St. Jude"*,
Patron Saint of hopeless cases, lost causes
And the impossible, including scarecrow
Totems of contemporary England, scapegoats
For hyperbolic coigners of 'Scroungeland':
NEETs, *CHAVs*, travellers, Gypsies, Roma,
Romanians, Bulgarians, *"scroungers"*, *"spongers"*,
WRAGs, Giro-Ghouls, Dubious Gentiles
And the burgeoning sub-breed of ubiquitous,
Undisguised Dole-Jude, the Welfare Jew,
Shadow-projected scapegoat and umbrage-
Magnet from the tabloid-subbed subconscious
Of the Shabby Gentile... And there are reports
Of clumps of *"scrounging"* clouds smudging
Over the chalky Downs, a refugee-migrant
"Swarm" amassing in coupon-clutching
Reinforcements off Dover, intent on a spot
Of *"benefit tourism"* (risking life and limb
Paddling across choppy waters on makeshift
Rafts or in rubber dinghies —all to *"take
Advantage"* of our *"over-generous"* welfare
Budget and bask in UK benefit sanctions!),
Scourge of Cumulus Nimbyus and Numpties,
In spite of rhetorical hoardings put up to repel
Inland-bound gales of rogue immigration,
To signpost that BRITAIN IS OPEN FOR PREJUDICE,
Xenophobia and Enoch Powell's unfinished
Business recalibrated by Bullfrog Farage
And his entourage aka blinkered UKIP...

6.

But what was *"St. Jude"*...? A muscular gale,
A mostly stormy rumour, a tempest
Composed of eighty per cent hyperbole,
The rest, a lot of hot wind, hardly a hurricane:
Some trees felled in Hampshire, a handful
Of fatalities, a couple of swept-up toupees,
And a commonplace occurrence
Of another rail line down for routine myth-
Maintenance —hardly a repeat of 'Eighty-
Seven... Hence our crumpling newspapers
Spruced up their Copy, ploughed a sough
Of elephantine headlines to heighten
The water margins: in such *"unprecedented"*
Times the news has to be BIG to grab
Historically short attention spans, for these
Are the 'biggest' times *since records began,*
And that October was the windiest October
Since records began... Let the slogan be:
Blame the Weather, Blame Labour... for
Not fixing the roof while the sun was shining!
(So Tory Austerity Tsars started 'fixing' it
While it was raining, having already nabbed
All the umbrellas for themselves while
Leaving *"the plebs"* exposed to a pelting)...

7.

Thus was *"St. Jude"* magnified to a Giant far
Bigger in print than in reality (our media
Moguls buoyed on ever-reliable Great British
Gullibility), as is the *"Scrounger"*-Ogre
Who ghosts Beveridge's beleaguered Five Evils —
Want, Idleness, Disease, Squalor, Ignorance,
Together with the post-Thatcherite bonus
Sixth: *Benefits Dependency* —ubiquitous
Bogeyman of neoliberalism: the flipped
Elephant in the jumbo boardrooms of corporate
Capitalism's periodically collapsing
Employment apparatus of Upsy Daisy
Supply and Demand, exploitable surpluses,

Cheap pools of unemployment to muddy
Bargaining for higher wages... And everyone
Knows a *"scrounger"* or knows someone
Who knows one, countless witnesses testify
To overhearing them bragging down the pubs
About how much they milk from the welfare
Teat while sinking pints and sucking vapes
(Not just at The Strangers' Bar); we're the nation
Unafraid to call a spade a spade,
We recognise a *"scrounger"* when we see one
(And even when we don't —snag their shadows);
Ogres of our ragman imaginations;
"Scroungers" are everywhere but are well-disguised,
Incognito, camouflaged germs, contagious...

8.
But Grand Guignol and rumour-mongering
Of mythological Copy sells as many rags—
Moguls guard jealously their Scroungerology,
So they'll keep stringing out astringent gossip
And malignant marginalia targeting
The marginalised, *"sponger"*-propaganda,
"Scrounger"-mongering, poverty pornography,
Welfare self-relief —as transposed to television:
Britain's Benefit Tenants; Saints and Scroungers;
Benefits Britain: Life on the Dole; Benefits Street
Etc. —a claimant-caricaturing
Cottage industry; they'll keep pouring out
Their poison and vitriol straight down our throats
Until our parroting mouths sprout thought-forms
With cloven hooves and *"workshy"* horns,
Striking Right-twisted attitudes
On plateaus of pack commonality, spice up
Copy till it's piquant with Scroungerphobic
Soupçon soaking up our lexicon, poisoning
The well of the welfare debate, muddying
The empathy-pool —then print, and keep printing,
To hypnotise grasping publics shopping for
The latest designer stigmas, brands and labels,
Until reality itself readjusts the facts

To suit the attitudes and narratives, succumbs
To print-hypnotism, media-Mesmerism,
Commercial Mendelism —no surer self-
Fulfilling prophecy than brainstorming taboos,
Projecting shadows over a Starbucks first
Thing in the editor's suite at the *Daily
Express*, hypnopompic red-top, Desmond's
Pseudologia published through Northern
& Shell's sleight-of-hand publishing group,
Press legerdemain, a meme-machine
Manufactured by Cagliostro & Sons —
A mechanical Pinocchio specially equipped
With dysphemistic typeset to punch out spontaneous
"Scrounger"-rhetoric, *"sponger"*-prop, sops
To put-upon proles who need dead dole-souls
Dropped into their morning red-tops in order
To feel superior in their despised employment...

9.
But for a slightly more 'upmarket' slice
Of crypto-fascist fiction with the sour bite
Of grapefruit in the morning, there's always
The *Daily Mailthusian*, inveterately
Anti-everything, except its own prolific
Prejudices rinsed in public through the greasy
Rothmere wringer of vicarious Viscounts,
Harmsworths of supplemental harm (old
Contemptible and intransigent right-winger
Of the mainstream British press, tub-thumper
For the Blackshirts as contrapuntal propaganda-
Organ to Oswald Mosley's *Action* in
The Thirties), polluter of public opinion
Through misanthropic Copy —trumped-up
Trumpeter of splenetic tripe, off-topic,
Personal manifesto of fear-and-loathing
Self-fellatio for its teeth-clenched editor,
Dummy-grimacing Dacre, spleen-venting
Ventriloquist of vile grievances, executive
Of invectives, Grand Vizier of the violet-
Dyed antediluvians and blue-rinsed housewives,

Who'll only give the green light to pitches
Which pass the acid test of his litmus paper;
Tsar of social scapegoating, *éminence grise*
Of light-touch self-regulation as Chair
Of the Editor's Code of Practice Committee,
An emphatically separate body to the Press
Complaints Commission in whose shell-likes
It whispers points on protocols, rendering
The other mute (the mouth of the *"toothless"*
PCC is parsecs past cosmetic dentistry —
While IPSO (the Independent Press Standards
Organisation) tiptoes into operation
But is ipso facto promptly compromised
By the omnipresence of Paul 'Muckspreader'...

Daily Mail "Hurrah for the Blackshirts" by Viscount Rothermere

10.

But even the more 'respectable' supplements
Of bowl-scraping moral panics scoop up
An unpalatable helping on the runcible spoon
For soup-sipping blue-rinsed readerships,
As Dacre discovered, to his sour taste,
After his paper's splash on 'Comrade Ralph',
Ghost father of the then-Leader of the Opposition,
And its poorly-concealed spicing with anti-
Semitic piquancy, proboscis-scoped scoops
Probing both father and son's 'suspect' tap-
On-the-nose associations ('Communist' as code
For 'Jewish' —always a double bugbear for Karl Marx):
Antediluvian déjà vu straight from
Disraeli days, though now *"One Nation"* is no
Longer blue but more a shabby aubergine
For Bourgeois Labour) —rightly, a public outcry
Ensued, including from among *Mail*-subscribers
Suddenly appalled at their own deep-seated
Prejudices: the openly persecutory tone
Of a newspaper they'd so long supported,
Whose graphically discriminatory take on
Practically any topic they'd not spotted
Until now: so shocking that Rothmere's rag —
Which once danced to the tune of the British
Union of Fascists— should stoop to such
"Unacceptable" anti-Semitic tittle-tattle
(Which should have been diplomatically kept
In the supplemental back pocket)! Yet
Scrounger-mongering of the economically
Disadvantaged seems acceptable, since
Unemployment's deemed *'unacceptable'*,
Not from the compassionate point of view
That it's a shameful waste of human potential,
But simply that it's a waste of *"hardworking"*
Taxpayers' money to fund all the claims for
State assistance from those out of work,
Whose doles are disparaged as *"handouts"* —
Giros granted to those gratefully tagged
With stigmas, invisible badges of shame...

11.
Anti-welfarism's one thing, anti-Semitism
Another entirely —even if the same tone
Of language and logic of argument are used
In both cases; stigmatisation of single
Mothers on benefits, greased in eugenics
Terminology, calls for a capping of babies
Wrapped up in giro-nappies, *"scrounger"*-
Hounding, red top columns recommending
Claimants be denied the vote (and ipso
Facto full citizenship —as with prisoners),
Stripped of benefits and chucked coupons
For food banks, or special payment cards
To police their purchases and more visibly
Single them out in public as examples
Of an unproductive sub-species —is all
Seen as fair game; to verbally brutalise
A minority on the basis of race or religion
Is —*rightly*— taboo (except for immigrants,
As supplemental pogroms on Roma,
Romanians, Bulgarians and Albanians
Prove) —but to verbally brutalise a minority
On the basis of economic circumstances,
Whether temporary or longer term, simply
Because they claim some state assistance,
Seems deemed to be perfectly compatible
With our much-trumpeted *"compassionate"*
And *"tolerant"* national character;
You shouldn't persecute those who haven't
Chosen to be Chosen; but the unemployed
Choose unemployment —so the red-tops
Spoon-feed to us on a bread-and-circus basis,
And expenses-fiddling, second-home-flipping,
Taxpayer-ripping MPs expressly impress
Upon us, so it's permanent open season
For press-persecution of the unemployed
As *"parasites"* —fleas of unearned leisure;
Stigmatising strugglers as *"scroungers"* is
Judgemental England's guiltless pleasure...

12.

Newspapers make up news, cultivate our views;
Shape and manipulate factual parameters,
Cheapen polemic with swipes and smears;
Reciprocate cut-and-paste public 'opinions'
Sculpted from warped dominions
Of lampblack columns; disrupt our capacities
For rational thought with well-placed spikes
Of opprobrious tropes signposting new types
Of *'taxpayer-sapping parasites'*
(Excepting our politicians!); punching
Buttons of phobic compulsions to spice up
Spiked Copy; fruitfully intrude on our
Flights to reflection through feedback from
The tuning-forks of their reflexive views,
Spoonfuls of offal from glorified rags
Of gossip-pimping, gormandising moguls
And oligarchs of our Murdochracy —yellow
Journalism's a gutter game of grimy origami:
Sculpting paper scapegoats to soak up the blame
For our umbrages and gripes: red herrings ripe
For pins of our spite, nailing up on public rood:
Each disposable red-top needs a disposable Jude...

A Modest Proposal by the DWP

Headline: "HYPERBOLIC RESPONSES" TO THE DWP'S POLICY PAPER, 'A MODEST PROPOSAL FOR PREVENTING THE SICK AND DISABLED FROM BEING A BURDEN TO THEIR COUNTRY...'

Blank defends Blank after he likens DWP cuts to the disabled to efforts of Nazi dictator

Blank: "Hitler and various people tried this out. The DWP work capability assessments and disability cuts are an attempt to do this by different methods."

Blank has backed Blank's claim that the DWP has the same goal as Hitler in trying to wipe out the sick, disabled, mentally ill, those unfit for work and those deemed "economically unproductive", despite the DWP branding the comments "offensive and desperate".

The former Blank drew criticism on Saturday after making the link between the DWP and the Nazi dictator Adolf Hitler in a newspaper interview. While Blank acknowledged the DWP was using "different methods" to the Nazis (e.g. benefit cuts, sanctions, rigged assessments and the bedroom tax), his incendiary comparison quickly enraged government supporters.

In an interview with the *Sunday Torygraph*, Blank, seen as the de facto leader of the No to Assisted Dying Coupons for the Disabled campaign (NADCD), said the past 2,000 years of European history had been dominated by doomed attempts to eugenically or administratively cleanse the physically and mentally unfit, to reinvent the more brazen practice of the Ancient Greeks and Romans who routinely abandoned disabled children on cliff tops to the mercy of the elements.

"Draco, Caligula, Nero, Domitian, Commodus, Attila the Hun... Hitler, from the Spartans to the Nazis, various people tried this out, and it ends tragically. The DWP is attempting to do this by different methods," Blank said.

"But fundamentally, what is lacking is the eternal problem, which is that there is no underlying moral argument for justifying the scientific logic of eugenics policy for the incapacitated. There is no single argument that anybody respects or understands. That is causing this massive moral void."

Blank, the former shadow work and pensions secretary said Blank's interview was "an abomination".

Condemning Blank's "slandering" of his time as head of the DWP and architect of the toxic bedroom tax, and use of "historical parallels", Blank said: "He talked about this idea that somehow I was responsible for driving some kind of eugenics policy against the sick and disabled for purely economic purposes. This is untrue: I've done so out of a deep sense of compassion. It might not be 'politically correct' to broach this, but if we're all honest with ourselves, there does need to be some sort of final solution to the perennial societal problem of malingering incapacity. That's partly why I contracted Atos Solutions to carry out the work capability assessments: the clue is in the name!

"It's a historical fact of life that if you go through Lloyd-George, Keir Hardie, Attlee, Bevan, Corbyn, everyone else ... I think the whole process of trying to support the sick and disabled through the welfare state and a bureaucracy of bleeding hearts is just prolonging the agony, that we as humanity just have to get to grips with the problem of over reproduction of the crippled and mentally afflicted and conflate it through legislation with a reciprocal chronic under consumption among such groups which will inescapably but necessarily wipe them out for their own good".

Responding to the comments, the current work and pensions secretary, Blank, said: "Disability campaigners might have won the moral argument but they are losing their economic compass. "After the second world war, the welfare state helped to perpetuate the economically unproductive longevity of the sick and disabled, trapping the crippled in a vicious life cycle which was of no benefit to them or anyone else, and was copied in social democracies across Europe. But for Blank to make the comparison between the DWP cuts to disability and the Nazis is deeply offensive: the Nazis wiped the sick and disabled out for pure hatred and expediency, we are wiping them out from a sense of compassion..."

Salted Caramels

Garthwaite, K. (2014) 'Fear of the brown envelope: exploring welfare reform with long-term sickness benefits recipients.'

"Authorised Systematic Harassment has enormous potential. The slow and noiseless steamroller of the State. The daily brown envelope dropping on the mat"
—Wilfred Greatorex, *1990*

"The Tories have weaponised welfare" —Jonathan Bartley, Green Party

The DWP —Department for Weapons and Poisons—
Deploys a plethora of paper weapons against the unemployed, Origami
games galore down at jobcentrepluses
These days, administrative harassment of claimants,
"Disrupt and upset" is the protocolic sport,
Managers cutting out cardboard sheriff badges
To pin on employees' lapels for hitting targets
Of sanctioning sundry jobseekers for missing
Post-dated appointments too prompt for the post
(Brownie points for brownouts) —but there's
No excuse for poor clairvoyance among
The *"scrounging"* classes, it's just another type
Of avoidance of work or looking for work
(Even if most vacancies advertised are fictitious!),
Taking up unpaid placements or internships;
There's Customer Compliance appointments
Elliptically phrased in sterile letters that leave
Much space for doubt and dread for recipients
As to what to expect on attending 'tape-
Recorded' interviews —lie detectors, thumbscrews,
Piano wires (for the Caxton House Gestapo)...?
Nothing so three-dimensional, for it's a game
Of malignant origami the DWP plays,
It prefers paper weapons —O, ink can kill as well:
An average letter from this Department can work
A pretty lethal spell of unsympathetic magic,
Like black spots to Black Dogs! But of all

The paper weapons deployed none compare
To brown envelopes, brown envelopes everywhere,
Ubiquitous brown envelopes, lying in baiting
Wait on doormats of a morning like paper moths
Or flattened preying mantises to greet indigents'
Lockjawed yawning; and these tan envelopes
Paralyse on sight, as soon as claimants spy them
In hallways they get dreadful frights, muscles
Tighten, throats turn dry, palms go clammy,
Brows perspire, hearts start thumping, pulses pumping —
Such symptoms these simple shapes inspire,
No mere rectangular gestures of tan paper
With glaring white fangs for windows sitting on
Doormats of the lumpenproletariat,
Simply petrify, sealed and pressed with spite,
Vituperative envelopes, primed paper weapons,
Packets of seeds to excite nervous dispositions,
Itch hypersensitivities, trigger anxieties,
Spring traps of panic attacks, fight-or-flights,
Make grown men quake over cornflakes —there's no
Escape from brown envelopes for recipients
(Except, perhaps, suicide —and O how many more
Suicides to be swept under the carpet by
Tampered DWP statistics, while particular cases
Still come to light, like Reekie, Clapson, Salter...?),
As long as someone's unemployed or
Incapacitated, day and night they'll be stalked by
These vicious missives, razor-sharp verdicts,
Tan fiends, buff furies, beige besiegers, brown
Plebiscites, salted caramels, salted with spite —
Not as butterscotch-sweet as *Werther's Originals*,
Nor even Beveridge's *"Five Giant Evils"*
Lozenge variety and lacking the glucose
Shots of Lloyd-George's *"Four Spectres"* —
Interminable brown robins with stark black
And white insides of menacing nomenclature,
Kafkaesque Doublespeak and implicatures
Paving the way to disinfecting sunlight
Like shards of burnt glass, to snip at and grate away
Fragile minds; some choose to eat them, so pretend

They haven't received them, but those who do
Will taste manila gum on gluey tongues and the bite
Of sodium chloride, for these are spiked repasts,
Bitter sweetmeats, unjust desserts laced with darnels —
The Department for Work and Pensions slowly
Poisons its claimants with salted caramels...

Claimant Christ

You've been seen out healing people
While your claim was still live
And you didn't declare the fact
Of raising Lazarus on the side —
But it's evident you are clearly
Capable of miracle-work...

So say you...

Don't obfuscate Mister Christ, it's clear
You're more than capable of work...

I never denied it...

Yet you don't
Declare your miracle-working!

I cure the sick in return for bread,
Man must make bread to keep alive...

Exactly! This is undeclared earnings!

No; it is a simple gift of sustenance,
Not Caesar's coin palmed on the hand —
See, my palm is empty but for a map
Of lines; rivulets on the skin's surface;
From many streams come rivers...

Yes, rivers of undeclared earnings...

The bird does not declare; it sings;
The lamb does not declare; it bleats...

OB-FU-SCA-TION Mister Christ —you have
Declared yourself unfit for work
And so receive sickness benefit

Yet your daytime miracles contradict this!

I did not declare that I was sick,
My Doctor did...

But you didn't deny it...?

How can I deny what I haven't said?

Don't get all Socratic with me Mr Christ!
You're being evasive —don't obfuscate...

No; it is the system works
To obfuscate entitlements
Through loopholes, while the Government
Scapegoats the struggling while it shirks
Responsibility for the vulnerable —
The world is ruled by fiddled numbers
And prating loss adjusters...

Let's see what your Doctor wrote about
Your contentious 'incapacity':

What he wrote was as dust on sand...

Well that's as maybe but it's in his hand —
And please, NO MORE APHORISMS! —
He's signed you off as chronically unfit
For manual tasks, arithmetic,
And all forms of office work...

I've never been good with numbers...

No, you couldn't correctly count up
The food bank coupons you conjured up
Apparently from thin air for that mob
Of homeless beggars...

It was a fair few...

FIVE THOUSAND, Mister Christ! ...But to
Return to the psychiatrist's report:
He writes you might be schizophrenic,
He recommends you to a clinic —
And did you take up the appointment?

Yes...

Don't be evasive, Mister Christ...

I say yes...

And what was the psychiatrist's verdict?

That I suffered from a psychotic delusion...

Ah, which is?

That I'm the Son of God...

Is that what you said?

No; HE said so, or implied it...

But why? You must have given him
A reason to make that diagnosis...?

I give no reasons to others' verdicts...

No more aphorisms or apothegms!
No more gnomic utterances!

*I simply sat there and when he asked me
If I was the Son of God I remained
Silent...*

A TACIT admission then?
You didn't deny it...? Interesting...

Why should I deny what I haven't said?

Did he mention other delusions?

Yes: that I have conquered death...

Well, good for you, Mister Christ...
Because he writes here that you claim
To have risen from your own tomb..?

I claimed no such thing...

                  Ok, then:
He PUT IT TO YOU that you thought you had?

Yes; but I didn't claim it...

But you didn't deny it..? Ok, Mister Christ,
As long as you can get a chit
From this trick-cyclist
Every three months you'll still receive
Your incapacity benefit...

I did not ask for it...

And yet you need to eat... to live...

I do not take, I only give...

So say you, but you're quite content
To take your weekly benefit...

I receive it, it is YOU who gives it;
I do not ask for it...

              So if we sanctioned
You how would you survive do you think?

Consider the ravens...

I already have,
None of them have ever done a decent day's
Work in their lives, the lazy scavengers...

Now I shall depart, but will return,
And you may keep my claim alive...

(*Sighs*) Don't worry, you'll get your dole...

I worry more for your immortal soul...

And what pray tell will you be up to
While you're away...?

I will atone for you...

Sign here Mister Christ...

I forgive you...

...and date it...

For you know not what you do...

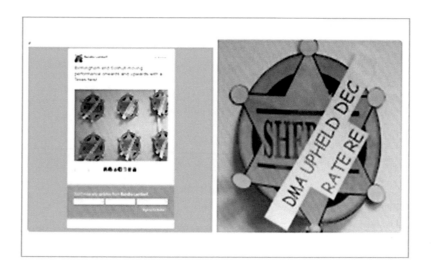

WORK

WORK, even when there's no WORK to be done,
WORK, WORK, so the mind doesn't come undone,
WORK, WORK, WORK, until the tired setting sun
Downs tools on dusk's brindled scaffolding, un-
Burdened of its whistling dromedary; dun-
Coloured of face, emitting sweet hum
Of endorphins' beatific fulcrum —
Sweatshop perfume: dirt-doctored talcum,
Combo of spent sweat, rank armpits, scum
Of dignity's dirt, fluid labour stung
With the fish-stink of soldering, melting gum:
Industrial altruism's squandered cum —
The best thing about WORK is it's never done...

WORK, monosyllabic God, as is your
Singular noun, JOB —O hybrid tyrant,
O hyperbole of labour, O canting label,
O titular stirrup, O halter of our souls,
O troubled promulgator of its own troubles
Buoyed into ambrosia of pocketed Profit
Pulped through the press of sacrificial bodies,
Libations of sweat and blood on factory altars
To the slavish Anti-Christ of your Ethic,
Antinomian dogma and Calvinist edict:
Employment must be punishing, monotonous, abject —
Your worshippers bowed and cowed with rickets...

WORK, until your nerves are shot through
To a bow-backed, ricketed boogaloo
Of ambrosia'd numbness: you've paid your due
To Olympian Bosses who've capitalised you:
You, that most sacred of commodities, true
As the altruistic clank of a machine part, blue-
Collar component, wrought unit, queue
For a pension of sawdust and splinters and rue
Of rheumatic spasms, broke posture, ague

Of hard WORK, hard tacks, your coveted cue
To finally put your feet up for a brew
And bow out to something quite chronic, taboo...

WORK is good for the soul...
WORK instructs our morals...
WORK collects us together
And puts us down like tools...

WORK gives us the inalienable right
To castigate the skivers who blight
Our island factory's enshrined birthright
To enslave its' Left to enrich its Right...

You have to work to have money,
You have to have money to work —
To afford the clobber, the lunches, the first month
Without any pay —and slog like a Turk
Not so much for monetary but moral gain:
So you can stand up and say I *flog my labour,*
Disenfranchise myself for economic good:
And though I'm still struggling
I'm eligible for judging
Those spongers and loafers
Who sprawl on their sofas
Just because they won't martyr themselves like me;
The only morality is WORK;
There's only salvation through WORK:
Hell's there to yoke those who shirk.
Heaven's a vague promotion for the
Dire-waged drones of mortality...

WORK has made a holy relic
Of your dusted donkey jacket
Trussed up on a coat-hook bracket
A leathery scrag-end exhibit
Sanctified in scum and tacit
Verisimilitude like the carrot
Of your paltry payback packet

That dangled all your days of garret-
Gardening to end them static
As a caveat in a small-print bracket...

The slavery of your days, their profit;
The profit of their days, your obit:
He gave his labour, did his bit
To create wealth, or rather, profit
Fleeced from him —and with this spit
We baptise him, Idiot —
Thus speaks the self-made priestly culprit
From his feathered nested pulpit
Who inherited the smooth-palmed itch
Of avarice and arithmetic
That taught him to exploit a tip
To his advantage, sift the grit
From swelling fingernails, encrypt
His interests in the steaming pit
Of others' efforts —apparatchik
Of the capitalist's bankrupt spirit...

Work is whatever we say it is —
Nothing is work if it doesn't make profits —
Exploiting labour, making profits,
That's the only work there is...

The grafters victory is pyrrhic:
Burnt out into retirement's clinic,
Knackered as a cart-nag, takes the billet
Of a doctor's illegibly scribbled chit,
Incapacitated through capitulative
Cramp, instate as Arthur Ritick —
Then clamps the final golden cribbage
Of his past masters, bronzed, Pharaohnic,
Without a hint of the ironic
To sweeten his last mortal tonic —
A brew stewed through a dog-end tip,
Adulterated, weak, pathetic —
Their temerity is peripatetic
To call this punishment an *Ethic*...

Waiting for Giro

Wragdole: What we have here is a pale suggestion and we are
trapped by this piece of franked paper. And yet, in this intense
privation, one thing alone is clear. We are waiting for Giro to come.
Escrogurn: I don't seem to be able... (*long hesitation*) to budget.
Wragdole: That's hardly surprising, since this paper affords us
nothing. Worse than nothing: something. But not enough
something. It's just a token to acknowledge we ought to exist,
in some form or other. As ghosts.
Escrogurn: Worse. Ghosts don't need money.
Wragdole: It's perpetuity's stipend. It stretches our bones on the rack
of waiting.
Escrogurn: How depressing.
Wragdole: To every doley his little cross. (*He sighs.*) Till he signs.
(*Afterthought.*) And is forgotten. Until the next time.
That little cross to point us to our Post Office. We wait.
We are bored. (*He throws up his hand.*) No, don't protest...
Escrogurn: (*Indignant*) I wasn't about to...
Wragdole: ...we are bored to death, there's no denying it. Good.
Giro comes along and what do we do?
We squander it. . . In an instant a fortnight's budget will vanish and
we'll be broke once more, in the midst of nothingness!
Escrogurn: I was only going to say... I'm beyond it.
Wragdole: Beyond what?
Escrogurn: Boredom. (*Afterthought*). By now.
Wragdole: You and me both. Both you and me.
Under this fruitless tree.
Escrogurn: How long now do you think? How long?
Wragdole: How long is a piece of string?
Escrogurn: As long as that? It seems ages since...
Wragdole: I know...
Escrogurn: ...the last one...
Wragdole: Mmmm?...
Escrogurn: ....came.
Wragdole: (*Holding hand up as if halting a protest*).
No, there's nothing to be done...
Escrogurn: I know... I'm doing nothing...
Wragdole: ...until Giro comes...

Blood of the Dole

O in those lean-to Thirties under Uncle Stanley's
Tenure of austerity, there might have been
Such things as Parish Relief, Public Assistance,
The dreadful Means Test, which summoned legion
Unemployed men cap-in-hand to beg for
Begrudging eudemonia doled out by
Judgemental panels, but this was some time
Before the Welfare State proper was built
And knee deep in the Great Depression;
Of all those who were let down by the dismantling
Of the Land Fit for Heroes which turned out
To be just a paltry epithet with nothing
Concrete about it, all those who'd sacrificed
Their youths' best years for ungrateful King
And Country, who'd answered the call from
Cartouched Kitchener —*Your Country Needs
YOU* (another bloomin' epigram besides)—
Then found themselves betrayed, half-mad from
Gas, or shell-shocked, in crutches, amputees,
Or maimed, betrayed by the Government,
By the pinstriped politicians who'd kept
Their legs genteelly under desks while khaki
Contemporaries rocked at makeshift tables
In trembling dug-outs, mud and blood up to
Their armpits and raglan sleeves; these MPs
Now waged a peacetime war against the unemployed,
And those many army veterans among them,
And a pool of war-crippled uncompensated
Who could no longer muster strength to work
For a wage or get any state assistance to help
Maintain them and their families, wounded
Not only in body and mind but also in pride —
Pride of being able to earn their crusts in peacetime;
So much for stripes and medals —now they were
Ripe for the scrapheap, for being forgotten,
Brushed aside as a bankrupt economy almost

YOUR COUNTRY'S

DONE WITH
YOU

Collapsed on top of them, the unemployed
And incapacitated crushed underneath
At the very bottom of the deeply planted,
Damp pyramid of capitalism retrenching as
The arms trade was drying up... And there was
A terrible true story of an army veteran whose
Old soldier's pride could no longer take
The torture of watching his expecting wife
Whittled to a swollen-bellied wraith through
Punishing shifts at a draper's, growing old
Before her time, wrung out through drudgery
And domestic chores: word had it he slit his
Throat in front of his poor wife who was due
To give birth to their child only one month later —
What a trauma for her to witness this
Suicide of a man she loved who'd survived
The worst of the Front and all that the Picklehaubs,
Shells, gas and rat-tat-tatting artilleries
Could throw at him, all just to end up spluttering
His last over an empty plate at the kitchen
Table back home in the country he'd fought
To keep safe from harm; frantic, she fetched
A neighbour who tried to staunch the blood
Ebbing from her husband's jugular,
But it was too late for him, the self-inflicted
Wound gushing —except for one last gesture:
He grabbed his neighbour's hand, opened
Up its palm as if smoothing out some paper,
Then, with a finger dipped in the pool
Of his own blood managed one last scroll
Of disjointed letters, a last request,
A dying signature —but it wasn't his name
The letters spelt out: just simply 'D-o-l-e'...

Another Five Giants

'...*the true object of the Welfare State... is to teach people how to do without it*'
—Alan Peacock, *The Welfare Society* (1961)

'*Whatever temporary benefits may have accrued from welfare interventions may now, it seems, flow from the workings of unimpeded market forces, and the Welfare State should be allowed to wither away as speedily as possible. ...This particular point of view is... naively convinced of the primary importance of material incentives as a stimulus to activity, and fearful of the effects of welfare policies upon their recipient's moral fibre (with particular reference to his will to work)*'
—Ken Coates and Richard Silburn,
'The Decline of the Welfare State', *Poverty: The Forgotten Englishmen*
(Pelican, 1970/ rev.1973)

'*We have helped change the debate on welfare ... no frontbench politician is now using disgraceful, divisive terms like* 'scrounger', 'shirker' *or* 'skiver'. *They have been shamed by the reality of life ... for millions of our people in left-behind Britain. ...The injustices that scar society today are not those of 1945...* Want, Squalor, Idleness, Disease *and* Ignorance ...*they have changed since I first entered Parliament in 1983... Today what is holding people back above all are* ... Inequality ... Neglect ... Insecurity ... Prejudice ... *and* Discrimination...'
—Jeremy Corbyn, 2016

1.
In the hard-fought Forties, armchair reformer,
Fabian-influenced Liberal economist
And social hygienist, W.H. Beveridge,
Compiled a Report on the state of the Have-
Not nation, the unemployed and incapacitated,
Those minion millions whom in spite of Liberal
Interventions earlier in the century—
Of social insurance schemes and compensation
For spells of unemployment— still battled
Social diseases of under-consumption,
Malnourishment, rickets and consumption
Due to slum conditions, vitamin-deficient
Diets and poor sanitation, identifying
What he termed the *"Five Giant Evils"* —
Want, Ignorance, Disease, Squalor & *Idleness*—
That stalked the land; *and the greatest of these...*

2.

But there seemed something judgemental
In Beveridge's message: ambiguousness
In *Ignorance* which might have been signposting
Poor schooling *or* that some simply opted
To be ignorant; while *Idleness* seemed less
Ambiguous in its emphasis on behaviour,
As if to signal this particular *'evil'* was elective,
A voluntary vice, even a deviancy —
There'd been no such aura of judgement in
David Lloyd George's evangelical message
On alleviating poverty and unemployment,
Expressed as much by the poet in him as
The politician, with a spicing of the pulpit-
Rhetoric of the Baptist Minister: *"Four*
Spectres haunt the Poor —Old Age, Accident,
Sickness and Unemployment. We are going
To exorcise them. We are going to drive
Hunger from the hearth. We mean to banish
The workhouse from the horizon of every
Workman in the land" —thus roared the Welshman
From Llanystumdwy, laying four foundation
Stones for future efforts towards relief
Of proletarian distress, anti-totems
To be toppled and thence emancipate
And empower the poor; and here the emphasis
Was on things that *happened* to the poor,
Not on anything happening as repercussions
Of choices *made by* them —prescription as
Opposed to proscription; so the fundamental
Template for a state safety net to catch
And support the poorest, funded by taxes
On the better-off, was formulated and put
In place in spite of frothing opposition from
The entire British Establishment (the hoary
Goliath this David slew with his sling
Of oratorical stones); inevitably this 'net'
Had teething troubles, and would partially
Function in an underdeveloped, improvised

Fashion in its novice field of welfare relief,
Government-dealt dole under aims of eudemonia,
To be a long-term legacy of subsequently
Labelled *'bleeding hearted'* Liberals,
Those of a radical timbre almost singular
To the unrewarded dawn of the Edwardian era:
Campbell-Bannerman, Asquith, Lloyd George...

3.
Thirty years later, the rudimentary architecture
Of a future Welfare State still in scaffolding
Hard-fought for on behalf of the *"Four Spectres"*-
Haunted poor in 'The People's Budget'
Of 1909 that brought in private rent
Controls and dole for the unemployed
(Promptly stigmatised as *"going on the Lloyd
George"*, a signature that degenerated later,
Mutated into administrative hatred
And the punitive Means Test most notorious
In the Nineteen Thirties for humiliating
The disadvantaged forced to go caps-in-
Hands up against judgmental panels under
Stanley Baldwin's *'Two Nations'* Tories)
Was ripe for further development, for flesh
To be stretched over its' sketched skeleton,
Some gristle on the bones; and homburged
Beveridge, then a high-ranking civil servant,
Was the man tasked to compile a report
Making recommendations towards this:
He proposed a more comprehensive system
Of social security to tackle the Five
Evils he'd identified in his retrospectively
Eponymous Report —a system which was
Eventually built by the post-war Labour
Government under Prime Minister Clement
'Little mouse' Attlee (a veritable mouse
That roared) —once a small 'c' Conservative,
Who'd converted to Socialism lightning-
Struck during his Damascene-time as manager

Of Haileybury House, a charitable club
For working-class boys deep in the slums
Of Stepney... So was summoned in
Social security for periods of unemployment;
State pensions and national insurance
To compensate industrial injuries and other
Occupation-stopping incapacities;
A mass programme of council house building;
Nationalisation of major industries,
Utilities and public services; a Landlord
And Tenant Act to cement private rent controls,
And protect tenancies; and a National Health
Service free at the point of delivery —
All packaged together under the banner
"From cradle to grave", collectively termed
The Welfare State or Attlee Settlement...

SPITE SCROUNGER- STIGMA JUDGE- RESENTMENT
        MONGERING   MENTALISM

THE FIVE GIANT SHADOWS

4.
But this beneficent safety net has been steadily
Unthreaded through the decades post-'79,
The Welfare State gradually undermined
By successive governments leaning Right,
Under subterfuge of *"reforms"* slowly but
Surely letting in the wolf that welfare kept
From the door, amounting more to sabotage...
By the beginning of the 21st century,
Neo-liberalism had dealt its recumbentibus
To the British Left, Labour bowdlerised
And blued by Blair under banner of *'New'*,
And under his Government policies geared
Towards social engineering and *'nudging'*
Germinated, ministers instructed to *"Think
The unthinkable"* —and they'd be backed
Up by private sector trouble shooters,
'Problem-solvers', medical insurance bods
And psychiatric bounty-hunters, thus all
Parties' mutually beneficial agendas
Were legitimised; a covert induction
Of a new Occupational Health Doublespeak,
A semiotic corruption of therapeutic ethics,
To be taken up by medical and psychiatric
Practitioners, took place at a psychosocial
Conference in Woodstock, Oxfordshire,
2001, on the judgementally titled theme,
'Malingering and illness deception' —
All participants were linked to UnumProvident,
A US insurance company represented by
One John LoCascio, and supported by one
Mansel Aylward, author of *'Worklessness
And Health: A Symposium'* (amongst other
Atomistic documents), then chief medical
Officer for the DWP, who kept its shadowy
Workings ticking over quietly, tick-tocking
Toxically —the shadowy Aylward was key
To this politico-corporate conspiracy
Against the sick and disabled, helping

Politicians find ways of *'weeding out*
The workshy' —or, at least, those depicted
Thus in order to fit his hypothesis;
And sifted out entitlements to benefits
For the mentally ill whose invisible
Symptoms were the easiest to invalidate,
Perceived physical wellness weighted against
Psychical incapacity, and through calculated
Misappropriation of occupational
Health theory, found ways of coercing
The psychiatrically afflicted —through
'Psycho-compulsion'— back to work,
Some mythical work, tasking *'basket cases'*
To make wicker baskets (throw thy crutches
Away and walk on towards the *'work cure'*!),
Welfare-to-work, like clockwork, unpaid
Work placements, *not* exploitation because
The rewards were towards *'wellness'* (even
If penniless), work now caricatured as
A miracle cure for all ills including mental;
The other part of this putsch: a conspiracy
Hatched between politicians and the red
Top press to spread propagandist copy
Mythologizing an *"overgenerous"*
Welfare State greedily wrung dry by
A ubiquitous breed of gurney-malingering
"Scroungers", cripples *"on the fiddle"*,
"Spongers" in bandages *'swinging the lead'*...

5.
The so-called *'Waddell and Aylward Report'*
Was published in 2005, its actual title,
The Scientific and Conceptual Basis
Of Incapacity Benefit: it recommended
The disregarding of medical opinions
From claimants' GPs and consultants —
Sickness chits flipped paradoxically
To *'fit notes'* in the new Dee-Double-U-speak
Poisoning the phrasal pool of occupational

Health —and the use of a new *"functional*
Assessment" using the bio-psychosocial
Model; by 2007, ex-City banker
David Freud was appointed by the Government
To compile a report on welfare reform,
Duplicitously titled, *Reducing Dependency,*
Increasing Opportunity: Options for
The Future of Welfare To Work that claimed
It was possible and desirable to kick
A million sick and disabled claimants
Into indiscriminate *'work'* —a twisted
Notion of a *'work cure'*; forced off benefits
For any job on offer; a different approach
To the Diaspora of the incapacitated,
Mass asylum-exodus that marble Margaret
Imposed, psychiatric closures and clearances —
Euphemised as *'Care in the Community'*,
Which saw the mushrooming of street
Homelessness, an epidemic of rough sleeping
Particularly amongst the mentally ill,
Cut-out citizens of cardboard cities, in
The brutalising Eighties... Freud recommended
The Aylward-watered-down, medically re-
Circuited new work capability assessments
Of the sick and disabled be conducted
By publicly unaccountable private
Companies specialising in medical charlatanry
In return for bounties; in 2008,
The Government contracted French IT firm,
Atos Solutions, who rebranded the bogus
Unregulated wing of their enterprise as
Atos Healthcare (up until their brand became
So toxic that they had to opt for the more
Nondescript-sounding name, Independent
Assessment Services) —and the rest is,
Tragically, history of bureaucratic
Atrocity; Freud switched party allegiances
And was promoted to Parliamentary
Under Secretary of State for Welfare Reform

Under the new Tory-led administration
During which tenure he made such discriminatory
Recommendations as the disabled being
Put to work for £2 per hour for projected
Lower productivity —he made the perfect
Pinstriped quips to complement red-top
Tropes and spice the more spiteful and charmless
Dictums of truculent martinet Iain
Duncan Smith, menace of the nation's
Underclass and mythical curtain-shutters...

6.
But even from the very beginning there was
A red shadow emitted from the seemingly
Angelic architecture of the Welfare State,
A bruising underbelly to Beveridge's
Evergetism, which might make some of his
Disciples since —even the most devout—
Question his unquestioned secular
Canonisation, and chill them: earlier
In his career, Beveridge was a member
Of the Eugenics Society, and, in 1909 —
Ironically the same year that his party
In government introduced the radical
"People's Budget" (hailing which Chancellor
David Lloyd George wistfully prophesied
A time when poverty would be as distant
A memory as *"the wolves which once infested
Our forests"*) —he proposed that those who
Could not work should be supported by
The state *"but with complete and permanent
Loss of all citizen rights —including
Not only the franchise but civil freedom
And fatherhood"* —proposals to stop
The lumpenproletariat reproducing
In an attempt to —somewhat brutally— stamp
Out poverty and associated ills rather than
"Patching" up the problem with compassion
And supplementary benefits, an approach

Which, a century later, the political
Persecutor of the sick, poor and unemployed,
One-time Work and Pensions Secretary,
Iain Duncan Smith, transposed into capping
Child benefits after the third child, and wiping
Out tens of thousands of disabled citizens
Through rigged work capability assessments —
Actually covert invalidity vetting —
Carried out by bounties-incentivised
Pontius Pilate companies that found tens
Of thousands falsely *"fit for work"*, many
Of whom subsequently died within six
Weeks of the decision (inclusive of suicides),
Or were financially and psychically
Crippled under the scrimping auspices
Of the Department for Work and Pensions...

7.
Did the *"great"* Beveridge have an ulterior
Motive in his blueprint for bettering the lot
Of the unemployed and lumpenproletariat?
Was he compromised by a conflict of interest
Undeclared in his eugenics connections?
On the day the House of Commons met
To debate what later became known as
'The Beveridge Report', in 1943,
Its author *'slipped out of the gallery early*
In the evening to address a meeting
Of the Eugenics Society' where he was
Especially keen to *'reassure'* members
That his Report *'was eugenic in intent*
And would prove so in effect... The idea
Of child allowances had been developed
Within the society with the twin aims
Of encouraging the educated professional
Classes to have more children than they
Currently did and, at the same time, to limit
The number of children born to poor households' —
Something taken up just under seventy

Years later by DWP hatchet-man
Duncan Smith; *'For both effects to be properly*
Stimulated, the allowance needed to be
Graded: middle-class parents receiving
More generous payments than working-
Class parents'... From the outset, then,
The template of the Welfare State was self-
Gentrifying in terms of social-engineering,
Its' fundamental trajectory not so much
Towards eliminating poverty —O to solve
Insolvency!— as covertly sieving out
The poorest and the long-term unemployed —
"Weeding out the workshy" as Duncan Smith
Would phrase it at a far flung future date —
Pulling the lumpenproletariat up by their roots
And bootstraps, imposing a type of dampness
Through pecuniary means to cultivate
An atmospheric impotence in an attempt
To stop them reproducing, at least,
At then-current rates, capped benefits
Having the effect of fiscal contraceptives,
Reduced household budgets to reduce
Libidos by reducing energies through
Insubstantial diets, giros transfigured
As castrating agents of the state, copper
Pennies heaped in tins, sperms permanently
Arrested as tadpoles in frogspawn scooped
Up in jam jars from green-slimed ponds,
Reduced spending power, the ultimate
Passion-dampener, anti-aphrodisiac,
While precautions against reproduction
Became more cheaply priced, choicest
Bespoke options marketed by word-of-mouth
Under numerous European euphemisms —
Dutch Caps, French Letters, English Overcoats;
Eugenics incognito; pecuniary cull
Of the impecunious; material
Sterilisation of the underclass, Dutch-capping
Of the lumpenproletariat by stealth:

'The Home Secretary had that very day
Signalled... the government planned a flat
Rate of child allowance. But Beveridge
Alluding to the problem of an overall
Declining birth rate, argued that even
The flat rate would be eugenic.... (to reassure
His private audience) ...He held out hope for
The purists. *'Sir William made it clear
That it was in his view not only possible
But desirable that graded family
Allowance schemes, applicable to families
In the higher income brackets, be
Administered concurrently with his flat
Rate scheme'*, thus was it reported raptly
In the *Eugenics Review* at the time...

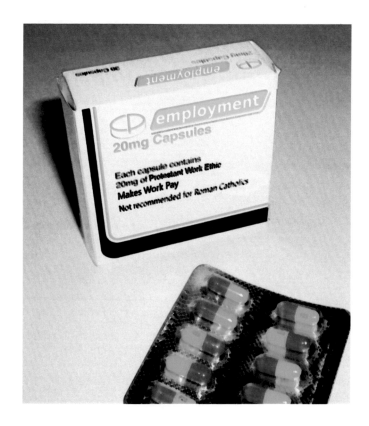

8.
Only sociologists in tortoise-shell glasses
Have been willing to interrogate Beveridge's
Regime of tough-loving paternalism,
See deeper through its' compassionate camouflage
Of gradualism that besotted
The bourgeoisie of an entire generation
Who'd entrusted him as fiduciary
With the allocation of their tax contributions
To best alleviate the distress of the poor,
Unemployed, depressed; but these forensic
Ethical criticisms took time to mature
And articulate, until by the early Sixties
Intellectual disillusionment was damply
Setting in with the Welfare State's self-
Immolating atomisation of its claimants,
Its inbuilt abuse of its own beneficiaries,
Policing and depletion of its dependents,
Aphorised by economist Alan Peacock in
The Welfare Society published 1961:
'...the true object of the Welfare State... is
To teach people how to do without it' —
Indeed, by the early Seventies, corduroyed
Social scientists, Ken Coates & Richard
Silburn, had diagnosed a faulty navigation
At the helm of the social security system:
That it was more on course towards charting
Maps of demographic damage-limitation
Than fundamentally alleviating
Material distress and levelling uneven
Grounds of intergenerational indigence,
Not so much about eliminating poverty
As ploughing through the poor —this was
The tall price of insisting on universalism
From the outset, projected to be the very
Thing that would galvanise public support
Across all classes, forge a consensus,
For a fledgling Welfare State and safeguard
Against its being attitudinally ghettoised

And subsequently stigmatised as something
Put in place purely for the benefit
Of the poorest (and thus most 'suspect');
And yet, paradoxically, it was precisely
This universalism which effected a sifting
Out through the safety net of those very
Families most in need of it, or, at best,
Keeping them in their place, for it in turn
Necessitated gentrifying welfare rates
And apportioning benefits pegged to station,
Rising in amount as one crept up the social
Scale, thus giving more to those with something
To spare, least to those with next to nothing,
And thereby expertly perpetuating
Material inequality: simply lifting up
The social edifice complete and intact...

9.
In 1970, Coates & Silburn already sighted —
And cited as a chapter heading— 'The Decline
Of the Welfare State', the withering
Of the benefits shrub in its fight to push up
Through the impermeable topsoil
Of capitalism: 'Whatever temporary
Benefits may have accrued from welfare
Interventions may now...flow from
The workings of unimpeded market forces,
And the Welfare State should be allowed
To wither away as speedily as possible' —
This is how they expressed the impatient
Capitalist point of view which they said
Was 'naively convinced of the primary
Importance of material incentives
As a stimulus to activity, and fearful
Of the effects of welfare policies upon
Their recipient's moral fibre (with
Particular reference to his will to work)';
Coates & Silburn argued that Beveridge's
Template for the Welfare State —soon after

Built by Attlee's administration— was
Perversely averse to alleviating
Material distress of the poorest during
Periods of unemployment or incapacity,
From the outset, perceiving financial
Generosity as potentially vitiating
Moral vitality, thus emphasis from the very
Start was on cast-iron conditionality,
And disincentives for perceived avoidance
Of the duty of earning one's living if able,
Or of conscientiously seeking work
When redundant, by dishing out sub-standard
Doles to the underlings of the social order,
Thereby also stripping the unemployed poor
Of any sense of self-respect whilst out
Of the employment market, in turn curtailing
Any temptation to state-dependence
(But also, paradoxically, shrinking the self-
Confidence of jobseekers crucial to successful
Re-procuring of employment): *'From the outset,*
The rates of benefit were too low to guarantee,
Even by Beveridge's own declared standards,
Security from want. ...Precisely in order
To avoid the situation where a family
Might receive more in welfare payments
Than it would in earnings, the Ministry
Operates a 'wage-stop'; ...Whatever level
Of benefits a family may be eligible
To receive according to the Ministry's scales,
The actual sum paid out shall not exceed
The amount that was being earned before
The interruption occurred'... So while the middle
Classes were incentivised to cultivate
Virility, have sex, and save (the state's key
Investments), the working and workless classes
Were besieged by ever more persuasive
Advertisements for contraceptives, taboo-
Lifted booms in abortions, and a state-
Generated indigence for which they were

Expected to show gratitude and a means-
Tested aggregate of guilt, and wear invisible
Badges of stigma, all for the grittiest privilege
Of being enabled to just about obviate
Absolute destitution: '...*the low wage-earner*
Can find relief neither as of right nor on
Demonstration of need, but must reconcile
Himself and his family to living at
Whatever standard his low wage permits.
This large group, who cannot escape poverty
While at work, can expect no improvement
In their circumstances in the event
Of a period of sickness or unemployment,
Which would make them eligible for both
Social-security and Supplementary Benefits.
...In the event of such low earnings being
Interrupted, the Ministry will fastidiously
Maintain such a family in its accustomed
Poverty: in no event can authority
Allow its resources to be used actually
To raise anyone's living standards, even
As far as the level of the Ministry's own
Estimate of minimum requirements' —This,
The apocryphal Pelican Gospel of Coates
& Silburn, immune to the most wool-pulling
Optimism of the post-war consensus:
Poverty: The Forgotten Englishmen —but
Not forgotten by them or their kinder ilk...

10.
Seventy-four years after the Beveridge
Report, seventy-one years after the start
Of the Welfare State, and thirty-seven years
After the advent of its gradual long-term
Dismantlement by administrations leaning
Right, two socialist pilots unexpectedly
Swept up into the cockpit of the Labour
Party tilting on its long-neglected left wing,
Corbyn & McDonnell, have defined another

Five Giant Evils for our time, marker-buoys
Of *"left-behind Britain"*: *Inequality...*
Neglect ...Insecurity ...Prejudice... and
Discrimination: *Inequality* in education,
Income, housing, life chances; *Neglect*
Of the elderly, the young, disabled, children,
Homeless, mentally ill; *Insecurity*
Of employment, renting, housing and health;
Prejudice against the poor, unemployed,
Disabled, mentally ill, homeless, immigrants,
Foreigners and refugees; *Discrimination*
Against the poor, unemployed, disabled,
Mentally ill, homeless, immigrants,
Foreigners, refugees and single mothers...
Everything progressive achieved between
The Forties and Seventies, during
The Attleean hiatus of the post-war
Social-democratic consensus —social security,
The cementing of private rent controls,
Nationalisation of industries and public
Services, greater worker and union rights —
Has been steadily eroded by destabilising
Rollerblades of banks-based economy,
The traumatic contractions of manufacture-
Crushing Thatcherism and its afterbirth,
The neoliberal incubus, the abolition
Of private rent controls and the privatisation
Of utilities and once-public services, boom
And bust, Buy-to-Let and sub-prime mortgages
Sent into tailspin on roulette-wheels
Of casino capitalism which collapsed
Into the banking crash of 2008
And eight years of fanatical austerity
Afterwards as an excuse to dismantle
The Welfare State and the last asthmatic
Gasps of the Attlee Settlement, strip it all
Down to scrap for private sector outsourcing
And subcontracting —all made acceptable
To an indoctrinated public on the back

Of blue torch-and-red top promulgated
Scroungermongering, and folkloric Rough
Musickings of prime cuts from a back-
Catalogue of gnomic numbers, vindictive
Non-movers, stigmatisation's Greatest Hits:
*"Something for Nothing", "Curtains Shut During
The Day", "Culture of Entitlement", "Culture
Of Dependency", "Culture of Idleness"* —time
To change the records? Spin a plate and see...

11.
Sprouting in the Welfare State's uprooted
Foundations, the pop-up post-society
Furnished with food banks, poor doors, homeless spikes,
Unpaid apprenticeships, zero-hours contracts,
Underemployment, corporate exploitation
Of the unemployed, discrimination against
All and any in need of state assistance,
Unaffordable spiralling private rents,
Diminished social housing, and from such ruptured
Ground sprang the new Five Giants, *fee-fi-fo-fum*,
Smelling the blood of forgotten Englishmen,
Congealing Englishmen... Now that Jeremy
And John have identified them we might
Eventually get to do something about them,
These evils deserving our attention, these
Deserving evils, before their planted feet
Root too deep into the lower stratums,
But in order to get into power to slay them,
Corbyn, labelled *"unelectable"* by everyone
Bar those who twice elected him as leader
Must get his heel-dragging party into government...
But —another *But*, and the most obdurate:
The balance of the ballot box depends upon
Opinions spoon-fed to the people by red tops
And purple supplements, the Tory and/or
Ukip-supporting newspaper opinion-shapers,
For it's not politicians who decide elections
But the popular press, prop of the powerful,

Opium of the newsprint-doped proles who are
Happily complicit in their own oppression
As long as they can have a few carrots thrown
At them now and then; the blue-rinse
Establishment's dyed-in-the-wool to its roots,
Roots that can't be moved, nor even shaken...

12.
The new Five Giants are formidable foes
Camouflaged against the intransigent glares
Of St. George flags in council house windows
Of forgotten Englishmen, empty-pocketed
Patriots who think they'll be spoilt for
Opportunities —once all the Polish fruit-
Pickers are packed off back to Poland— and
Not just for unpaid placements in *Poundland*;
And those soon-to-be-obsolete Butcher's
Aprons draped against sun-bashed glass
Of working-class amalgamates, angry glad
Englanders hoisting Agincourt salutes
At a Continent the British Isles turns
Its prickly backs to; Britain will be *"Great"*
Again according to jingoists Nigel and Boris,
Both notably absent during the mopping up
Of the diplomatic catastrophe once the plug
Had been pulled on our nation's forty-three-year
European experiment; the most monumental
Decision since entering the Second World War
Passed like the port by Pontius Pilate politicians,
Our appointed parliamentary representatives,
An invertebrate breed who chucked the bones
Of an incomprehensible debate out to
An information-deprived public through
A plebiscite, a public whose pool
Of opinions on Europe were poisoned by
Drip-fed red-top tropes and blue torch
Obfuscation, a Ukip-whipped *"People's
Army"* press-ganged by xenophobic pundits
And empurpled tub-thumpers, brainwashed

By immigrant-bashing tabloids, a nation's
Future put up for ransom because a mulish
Cabal of euro-sceptic Tories blackmailed
A spineless prime minister into holding
A referendum on a deeply complicated
Question with only the options of *"A simple*
Yes or No answer: Out or In" —and who,
Having lost, promptly tripped into the sunset
Of other enterprises, lucrative after-dinner
Speeches mopping up all the trimmings
And expenses, leaving behind a Britain well
And truly *"left behind"*, and rapidly sinking...

13.
The New Five Giant Evils have arrived,
And have been identified, but then they've
Been here for quite some time, just very
Well-disguised as lengthening shadows
Of Beveridge's original Five banished long ago,
As go bogus-progressive narratives,
But actually just scattered, still very much
Alive in spite of handpicked tsars' cherry-
Picking reports —woven into the worsted
Fabric of our culture, and sub-cultures,
Even *"Chav"*-adaptive fashionable label,
Burberry, a range from Selfridges, gets
'That Five Evils Vibe', patents and spins it
Into patterns of its five-tone synthetic
Tartan of the disadvantaged, checked skirt
Of the 'McChavish' Clan— too late to hack
The beanstalk back and catch the hatchlings,
The giants arrived some time ago and know
How many beans make five, those Ogmagogs
Gobbled up the golden eggs long ago,
And mythologized the state that lay them
As a profligate goose, its goslings as
"Scroungers" —but still kindling nostalgias
Regale the gullible round camp fires
Of self-sufficient futures where moral fibres

Are inextinguishable in the face of hardship
And have the foresight of squirrels to forage
And store for winter, and the stamina
To withstand the itch of indigence's
Stinging nettles without taking the swift
Relief of the dole cheque's dock leaf, since
Having one's benefits stopped and going
Hungry "isn't real suffering" in the silver-
Spooned opinions of minted Tory MPs (now
The wolves are infesting the forests again...);
They'll regale of the legend of gallant Sir
Beveridge chivalrously vanquishing
The Five Evil Giants from the land, even if,
Outside of fairy tales, he only marked them
Out, recommended some alms to armour
Their victims and the protection of a turret-less
Castle-keep tilting in on its' own built-in
Contradictions, the keep that expects
Its inhabitants to venture outside it and find
A more permanent refuge in self-help through
Personal enterprise, to fend for themselves,
No more beholden to spiky taxpayers
For unsympathetic support, begrudged
Contributions, hard-earned dog-ends for giros,
For there are far worse foes to face than
The Five Giant Evils, there are five ferocious
Fiends affiliated to their relief, five
Shadow evils vented by the devils
Of involuntary giving levied by governments
For meeting magnified targets of evergetism,
Exceedingly well-advertised altruism,
Penny-pinching arcade coin-pusher philanthropy,
Five evil reverbs with which every benefit
Recipient —in spite of evidence of deservingness —
Must learn to live, while trying to keep
Their self-respect intact; evils which are
Givens with receiving sieved victuals
We're forever told are diverted revenues:
Spite... Resentment... Stigma... Judgmentalism...

Scroungermongering... These are the five giant
Shadows thrown by the new Five Evils:
Irrespective of how *"deserving"* one's poverty,
Welfare is a flogging stool, benefits: taboos...

*   *   *

What have we achieved after the Attleean
Slaying of the Five Giant Evils of England?
After the lasting triumph of Thatcherism,
The neoliberal bribe, uncapped capitalism,
And the start of the dismantling of the Welfare State?

Another five giants have sprung up in place
Of Beveridge's originals, another five giants
Stalking the land and its stigmatised claimants —

Another five giants —fee-fi-fo-fum—
Smell the obsolete blood of forgotten Englishmen...

115

Notes to the poems

¡Viva Barista!
The title is a pun on *Viva Zapata!* (1954), title of a biopic about Mexican revolutionary Emiliano Zapata. **Kierkegaardian** refers to Danish philosopher Søren Kierkegaard (1813-55), specifically his *Concept of Anxiety* (1844). He is regarded as the first existential philosopher. A **demitasse** is a small cup used to serve Turkish coffee or espresso. **coffee-fetishism** is a play on Karl Marx's concept of *commodity fetishism*, which is:

As against this, the commodity —form, and the value— relation of the products of labour within which it appears, have absolutely no connection with the physical nature of the commodity and the material relations arising out of this. It is nothing but the definite social relation between men themselves which assumes here, for them, the fantastic form of a relation between things. In order, therefore, to find an analogy we must take flight into the misty realm of religion. There the products of the human brain appear as autonomous figures endowed with a life of their own, which enter into relations both with each other and with the human race. I call this the fetishism which attaches itself to the products of labour as soon as they are produced as commodities, and is therefore inseparable from the production of commodities.

(*Das Kapital*, 1867). This was developed further by György Lukács in his *History and Class Consciousness* (1923), in which he came up with the concept of *reification* (German: *Verdinglichung*, literally: *"making into a thing"*), the turning of abstracts into concrete objects, in this sense, the symbolic transposing of products into entities with personalities, as facilitated through advertising. Germane to all this is Karl Marx's theory of alienation or estrangement (*Entfremdung*) from the *"species-essence"* (*Gattungswesen*), as depicted in terms of how the human producer is simultaneously dehumanised and commodified as little more than a tool of a production process while the thing he produces is oppositely personified through copywriting spiel. Marx's famous aphoristic summation of religion —or, in his vocabulary, superstition— as *'the opium of the people'* (*'Die Religion ... ist das Opium des Volkes'*) is a phrase which also taps into his concept of commodity fetishism since —as Marx acknowledged in the above excerpt from *Das Kapital*— he derived his use of the term *fetishism* in reference to Charles de Brosses' *The Cult of Fetish Gods* (1760), a materialist treatise on the nature and origin of religion, which originated the concept of fetishism in terms of reification of 'gods' into things, objects, totems, idols etc.

Common Music
Common Music, a near-anagram of Communism, was the original title for this book but one I ultimately felt was too prosaic.(**incompatible with grapefruit Like most fast-acting pharmaceutical Citruses**): grapefruit juice apparently interacts negatively with certain antidepressants. **Fromm**, Erich (1900-80): Swiss-born German psychoanalyst, his concept of *'fear of freedom'*, divided into the negative *'freedom from'* (i.e. from interference by authority and convention) and the positive *'freedom to'* (i.e. to express oneself or exercise free will without

limitations), in his dialectical work *Escape from Freedom* (or *The Fear of Freedom*, 1941) concerns the human desire for certainty and security which can translate as a need to escape from freedom in some sense, which Fromm deduced manifested in three different human personality types: the authoritarian, the destructive and the conformist. Here Fromm's concept also links into the succeeding allusion to Keirkegaard and his aphorism on the nature of anxiety, *'the dizziness of freedom'.*

This poem is essentially about the rise of fascism at times of recession and austerity, as it rose in the 1930s, and as we are sadly witnessing once again today, in the UK, on the Continent, and in the US. The poem is consciously written in an Audenic style and tone befitting the theme. Many might think the West already has its **strong-armed conductor** in President Trump. Fascism comes camouflaged before it finally feels confident enough to break cover and display its more uncompromising full uniform; it starts with a trickle down of state- and newspaper-sponsored scapegoating of vulnerable minorities —e.g. the unemployed, refugees, immigrants— and such 'politically acceptable' prejudices in turn influencing public attitudes (e.g. the hostile treatment of sick and disabled claimants through the DWP-Atos WCA regime was made publicly palatable by Government and red top promulgation of the 'scrounger' meme). Immigrant-scapegoating, compounded by Theresa May's 'hostile environment' policy when at the Home Office, and the subsequent EU referendum made toxic by Nigel Farage's scaremongering about imminent refugee deluges, emboldened Far Right groups and movements: UKIP, the EDL and Britain First have become more vocal, and threaten to be even more so post-Brexit, seeing their hitherto proscribed xenophobic opinions as somehow licenced now. Our current MPs seem to think they can appease such poisonous attitudes in society by pushing through with Brexit, dangling the spectre of a phantom 'mob' to the rest of us as their last-ditch negotiating card, even though it spells catastophe for the country. This method is not only utterly spineless, morally bankrupt and politically inept, it is also doomed to failure, as the extreme Right is never satisfied and probably won't ever be until every last immigrant, refugee and foreigner has been deported from our shores. '**O those rose petal petitions that fall On deaf ears... scratched out by thornier Rhetoric, snagged on barbed remonstrations, Or cut down in frantic acts by radicalised Maniacs, suburbanite extremists**' alludes to the tragic assassination by a deranged Far Right/ 'Brextremist' constituent of Labour MP Joe Cox during the febrile EU referendum of June 2016 —**There's more that unites Than divides us** was a trope she used during a speech in Parliament.

The Battle of Threadneedle Street
Zimniy Dvorets: The Winter Palace (Russian: *зимний дворéц*) in Saint Petersburg, Russia, was, from 1732 to 1917. **Camels in flannel suits commute back through The needling eye of Threadneedle Street...**: allusion to Christ's proverb in Matthew 19:24: '...it easier for a camel to pass through the eye of a needle than for a rich man to enter the kingdom of God'.

Wood Panel Parliament
Kleisthenes: the founder of original democracy in Ancient Athens c. 508 BC.

Not Paternoster Square
Most allusions in the first two verses relate to the City of London Corporation, an opaque, shadowy ancient English institution dating back to Saxon times. It essentially owns the City of London (i.e. the 'Square Mile'), inclusive of Westminster; collects tax revenues from its residents; practices occulting symbolic ceremonies and processions (including the Lord Mayor's); has questionable connections with the finance sector; and has its own representatives in Parliament, such as the **Remembrancer,** lobbyist on behalf of the CoLC, who sits opposite the Speaker serving as permanent reminder that the CoLC's 'interests' must be borne in mind at all times. The CoLC is the nation's 'oldest continuously-elected local government authority', which is a roundabout way of saying that it is not elected; its powers and lack of transparency are criticised by many as anti-democratic. **costermongers, Cutpurses**: archaic terms for street-hawkers and pickpockets. **Cadastral**: (of a map or survey) showing the extent, value, and ownership of land, especially for taxation.

Portcullis Corporation is to emphasize the CoLC's 'occupation' of Parliament. **Ruritanian** see Notes to *RU-RI-TANNIA!* below. **The Duchy of Grand Fenwick** is a tiny fictitious antiquated country bordering Switzerland, France and the Alps, in Leonard Wibberley's satirical novel *The Mouse That Roared* (1955). **Camberwick Green** was the first of the Trumptonshire trilogy of stop-motion animated children's series, first broadcast in 1966 but repeated throughout the Seventies, as were its sequals, *Trumpton* (1967) and *Chigley* (1969). Sir Charles Asgill, 1st Baronet (1713–1788), merchant banker, was Lord Mayor of London during 1757-8, for whose inauguration the Lord Mayor's carriage —which is still in use today— was originally made; Asgill is an ancestor on my father's distaff side. **Candlewick Ward** is one of the 25 ancient wards of the City of London that come under the auspices of the CoLC. **Whittingtons:** *Dick Whittington and His Cat* is the English folklore surrounding the real-life Richard Whittington (c. 1354–1423), wealthy merchant and later Lord Mayor of London; according to the tale, Whittington rose from pauper to Lord Mayor of London through the selling of his cat to a rat-infested country —the definitive rags-to-riches story. *Sui oblitus Commodi: Forgetful of his own interest*: motto of the Asgills. *Something will turn ups* alludes to the phrase often used by the indefatigably optimistic shabby-genteel clerk, Wilkins Micawber, in Charles Dickens' *David Copperfield*. **Gradualist** refers to gradualism, theory that changes come about gradually, and is here contrasted with Fabianism, a gradualist socialist principle which believes political and social change comes about gradually through reform rather than suddenly and violently through revolution (Fabianism was named after Quintus Fabius Maximus Verrucosus (c. 280–203 BC), a Roman statesman and general of the third century BC, whose nickname was **Cunctator** meaning *'delayer'* for his tactics against Hannibal in the Second Punic War whereby he gradually wore down the Carthaginians by targeting their supply lines and engaging in small guerilla skirmishes against them).

képi blancs: French for *white caps*, referring to the caps covered with white cloths worn by the French Foreign Legion in the late 19th/early 20th centuries. *Topee neck curtains*: *topee* or *topi* was the pith helment, sun helmet or foreign service helmet worn by European colonial troops in the late 19th and early 20th centuries; sometimes, as in the case of the Sudan campaign of 1898, with a cloth that protected the nape of the neck. **Glossolalia**: *'speaking in tongues'*, a vocal phenomenon thought to represent the original universal language (of God) pre-Babel, sometimes witnessed in evangelical Christian gatherings. **Diggers**: an egalitarian social movement of the late 1640s/early 1650s which, in protest against private property and with a biblical conviction that the land belonged to all, set up communes at various locations throughout the country where they attempted to till —or *dig*, hence their name— unused land and grow their own crops to sustain themselves; all such communities were violently evicted by the Cromwellian militia. **Levellers** campaigned for male suffrage and a *'levelling'* of the land (i.e. equalising of rights), symbolised in their habit of trampling hedgerows (symbols of the Norman *'land grab'* and subsequent feudal system).

Nosterity: amalgam of nostalgia and austerity. **Pecksniff, Quilp and Heep**: three devious and manipulative antagonists in novels by **Charles Dickens**: Seth Pecksniff, unscrupulous charlatan architecture *'mentor'* who steals his students' designs (*Martin Chuzzlewit*, 1844); Daniel Quilp, grotesque usurious money-lender (*The Old Curiosity Shop*, 1840); and Uriah Heep, unctuous, calculating lawyer (*David Copperfield*, 1850). **Untermenschen**: *'underman'* or *'subhuman'* in German, the opposite of Friedrich Nietzsche's *Übermenschen* (*'Supermen'*), the *untermensche* was the collective pejorative term for all those deemed *'inferior'* or *'undesirable'* in Nazi society (e.g. Jews, the unemployed, the disabled, gypsies et al); the term was first used by American white supremacist Lothrop Stoddard in his 1922 book *The Revolt Against Civilization: The Menace of the Under-man*. **Brobdingnag**: the second country Lemuel Gulliver visits in Jonathan Swift's *Gulliver's Travels* (1726; 1753), inhabited by giants, by contrast to the first country he is shipwrecked on, Lilliput, inhabited by thumb-sized people (Lilliputians). *RURI-TANNIA*: see Notes to *RU-RI-TANNIA!*.

Haw-Haw: William Joyce (1906-46) aka 'Lord Haw-Haw', was an Anglo-Irish Fascist politician and Nazi propaganda broadcaster to the United Kingdom during World War II who was the last person to be executed for treason in the UK. Brian Haw (1949-2011) pitched a one-man protest camp against war in Parliament Square from 2001-6. **by Jingo**: this phrase originated in a song by G. H. MacDermott (singer) and G. W. Hunt (songwriter) commonly sung in British pubs and music halls around the time of the Russo-Turkish War (1877–78), the lyrics had the chorus:

> We don't want to fight but by Jingo if we do
> We've got the ships, we've got the men, we've got the money too
> We've fought the Bear before, and while we're Britons true
> The Russians shall not have Constantinople.

The phrase *"by Jingo"* was a long-established minced oath used to avoid saying *"by Jesus"*. Referring to the song, the specific term *"jingoism"* was coined as a political label by the prominent British radical George Holyoake in a letter to the *Daily News* on 13 March 1878 to mean extreme patriotism and aggressive foreign policy. *peasouper*: old-fashioned term for a thick green or yellow fog formed by pollution in cities. **variolation**: innoculation, first used against smallpox (*variola*). *"Invisible Hand"*:

The rich...are led by an invisible hand to make nearly the same distribution of the necessaries of life, which would have been made, had the earth been divided into equal portions among all its inhabitants, and thus without intending it, without knowing it, advance the interest of the society.

(The Theory of Modern Sentiments, Adam Smith, 1759): a highly dubious view that there are unintended social benefits that come about from individuals' self-interested actions, commonly used as a justification for capitalism and its mythical *'trickle-down'* effect. Claude Henri de Rouvroy, **comte de Saint-Simon**, often referred to as Henri de Saint-Simon (1760-1825), French political and economic theorist whose system of industrial critique which aspired to a more equal and productive society. **Kleptocratic**: state-sponsored theft. **a bubo of disembodiment; A pustule burst by buss of pecking proctors**: allusions to the Black Death/ Bubonic Plague (in the UK, 1347 to 1351 and 1666), bubo is a swelling of the lymph node, a common symptom, **buss** is kiss, **pecking proctors** refers to the plague doctors, also known as beak doctors for the beak-shaped masks they wore which were filled with herbs and spices to filter out the miasma of the plague thought to be its cause (though its actual cause was the spread of fleas from rats). **Stockholm syndrome** is a condition that causes hostages to develop empathy with their captors as a survival strategy during captivity.

Defenestrate: to throw something or someone through a window. *"Love the sound of breaking glass"* is apparently the motto of the Bullingdon Club, elite private all-male club for rich undergraduates at Oxford University, notorious for boisterous behaviours such as smashing up restaurants and vandalising student rooms as well as other egregious initiations such as burning £20 notes in the faces of homeless, which both David Cameron and Boris Johnson were members of while at Oxford. **Grantham and Finchley**: the former Lincolnshire town was Margaret Hilda Thatcher's (nee Roberts') birthplace, and the latter was her constituency in London when MP and prime minister.

prehensile: capable of grasping e.g. hand, claw or tail. **Carpocratian**: Ancient Judaic Gnostic sect, named after Carpocrates of Alexandria, who believed they could transcend the material realm and were not bound by earthly morality, and even thought breaking all moral laws was necessary for personal redemption; Carpocrationism was therefore a forerunner of *antinomianism*, a term coined by Martin Luther to denote extreme interpretations of his own doctrine: that salvation came through faith and divine grace alone (as in Calvinism), rather than through 'good deeds' (as in Arminianism), and that those who were *predestined* to salvation therefore had no obligation to conform to worldly law and morality (distortions of these credos arguably led ultimately to the transgressive ideas of the Marquis de Sade, Friederich Nietzsche, Aleister Crowley and Adolf Hitler). **Gorgonic**: relating to the Gorgons, female snake-haired creatures from Greek Mythology. **Methadone**: an opioid distilled into a green-coloured medicine which is prescribed to heroin addicts as a more innocuous alternative. **Absinthe**: concentrated alcoholic drink distilled from wormwood mixed with green aniseed which gives it its distinctive colour; historically the tipple of impecunious bohemians, particularly artists and poets, it was given the nickname *"la fée verte"*, the "the green fairy". **brown** meant here as a slang-term for heroin. **Vorticist**: pertaining to Vorticism, a short-lived avant-garde movement in art and poetry which championed abstract and geometric imagery focusing on the contemporary machine age, and announced itself with a manifesto in the first of just two editions of the magazine *BLAST* (ed. Wyndham Lewis, 1914).

Cyclops: one-eyed giants from Greek Mythology originally depicted in Homer's *The Odyssey*. **Tartarus**: a dark part of Hades (Hell) in Greek Myth. **Pompeian flea-pit of swingeing bites**: part-pun on Anglo-Scots poet James "Bysshe Vanolis" Thomson's melancholic long poem about London, *The City of Dreadful Night* (1870-80). *"Wrags"*: Work-Related Activity Group of Employment and Support Allowance. **Anarcho-Syndicalist**: a branch of anarchism that focuses on the abolition of capitalism through the organization of revolutionary worker syndicates. **Soylent**: a foodstuff surreptitiously made from human remains in the 1973 science fiction film *Soylent Green*, itself adapted from the 1966 novel *Make Room! Make Room!* by Harry Harrison, the name soylent being a portmanteau of soy and lentils.

Psychic Crimeas...ladies-of-the-lamplights alludes to Florence Nightingale (1820-1910) famously known as the 'The Lady with the Lamp', who introduced proper sanitation into field nursing during the war in Crimea (1853-6). **lobster-potted desecrators** alludes to the 17th century Roundheads, the Parliamentarian army formed to battle the King's in the English Civil War, who were so named partly because of their close-cropped haircuts which were thought to be very severe for the period as long hair was then in fashion, but also in part because of the rounded helmets they wore in battle which had plated rear-neck armour and gained the nickname of lobster pots or lobster-tailed pot helmets. The Roundheads were known to desecrate churches that had been redecorated and refurbished in line with the controversial reforms of Archbishop Laud, which installed, among other perceived Catholic-influenced features, altar rails that separated the priest from the congregation (symbolic of *sacerdotalism*: the belief that a priest is needed as spiritual intemediary between the believer and God), all of which Laud imposed uniformly nationwide and which thus incurred the wrath of the Puritans. **God-Builders** alludes to an obscure branch of the Russian Bolsheviks who promoted the reimagining of Communism as a secular religion with its own rituals, myths and symbolisms; the idea of *"God-Building"* (*bogostroitel'stvo, богостроительство*) was formulated by Anatoly Lunacharsk in his seminal two-volume work *Religion and Socialism* (1908–11).

Houdini, Harry (1874-1926), legendary Hungarian-born escapologist and illusionist. **Comptrollers:** here referring to the Comptroller of the High Officers of the City of London Corporation, responsible for provision of all legal services. The post of comptroller dates from 1311, and that of City Solicitor from 1544; the two were amalgamated in 1945 (from French compte (*"an account"*) and the Middle English *countreroller* (someone who checks a copy of a scroll, from the French *contreroule "counter-roll, scroll copy"*)). **Master of Ballentrae-cum-Ballentaylor**: George Osborne is heir apparent to the baronetcy of Ballentaylor in Ireland; he is here compared to the sinister and scheming James Durie from Robert Louis Stevenson's *The Master of Ballantrae* (1889). **Tobin:** a Tobin tax, suggested by James Tobin, an economist who won the Nobel Memorial Prize in Economic Sciences, was later adapted in the UK as the proposed Robin Hood tax, a package of financial transaction taxes aimed at redistribution to the poorest, particularly during the early days of Tory-driven austerity. **Thaxted Rectors**: Conrad le Despenser Roden Noel was a Christian socialist/communist Anglican vicar nicknamed the *"Red Vicar"* of Thaxted' (in Essex) for controversially hanging the red flag and the flag of Sinn Féin alongside the flag of Saint George in his parish church. ***Erskine May*** is the name of Parliament's rulebook, named after its original author, Thomas Erskine May (1915-86). *Hansard* is the name of the ongoing archive of transcripts from all parliamentary debates and speeches, named after its original editor/printer, Thomas Curson Hansard (1776–1833).

Diogenes Club: a private London club where misanthropic gentlemen sat smoking or reading their newspapers in complete silence, often frequented by Sherlock Holmes' older brother, Mycroft. **Norwegian outposts** is a reference to the sight of the Norwegian flag left at the South Pole by Roald Amundsen which greeted Robert Falcon Scott and his doomed Antarctic expedition of 1912, signalling that they had been beaten to the destination.

Jack Cades, Watt Tylers, Dick Turpins: Walter "Wat" Tyler, leader of the 1381 Peasants' Revolt, tricked by Richard II and slain by one of his henchemen on 15 June; Jack Cade was the doomed leader of a rebellion against the weak and unpopular Henry VI; Richard 'Dick' Turpin (1705-7—1739) was a famous highwayman and folk figure, in many ways a kind of 18th century Robin Hood, he was eventually caught and executed for horse theft. *hoi polloi: 'the many'.* **demos**: *'people'*, both from Ancient Greek. **evergetism** or euergetism (from the Greek εεργετέω, *"doing good deeds"*) was the ancient practice of high-status and wealthy individuals in society distributing part of their wealth to the community.

Nimbyish: from the acronym NIMBY: Not In My Back Yard. *"NEET"*: Government acronym for *'Not in Employment, Education or Training'*. **Yellowed Judases betray Him and his kind For thirty pieces of silver legislation Glimpsed against the sulphur plush of a closing Limousine door** alludes to the Liberal Democrats under Nick Clegg's leadership betraying millions of voters by going into 'Coalition' with the Tories in May 2010.

Gaunt's green-vaunted realm: alludes to John of Gaunt's famous 'this scept'rd isle... / ...this realm, this England' speech on the state of England in Shakespeare's *Richard II* (1595). **royal hunt of sunset Enterprise**: a triple allusion: *The Royal Hunt of the Sun* (1964), Peter Schaffer's play about the Spanish conquistadors' invasion of Peru, the massacre of the Incas, and their capture and eventual murder of their 'sun god', Atahualpa; **sunset** alludes to *'sunset clauses'*, cut-off dates for certain laws or regulations, often in business contracts, and also to the adage once commonly given to global empires, most recently to the British Empire: *'the empire on which the sun never sets'* —which was to say an empire was so vast-stretching that there was always one part of it in daylight at any given time. *Moai:* monolithic human figures carved by the Rapa Nui people on Easter Island in eastern Polynesia between the years 1250 and 1500, the huge bodies of which are buried in the ground while the iconic heads are visible; the statues still gazed inland across their clan lands when Europeans first visited the island in 1722. In hindsight, the heads really should be gazing inland in this poem by way of metaphor for our Brexit-reinforcing, inward-looking island mentality, though the poem was written back in 2011 when the EU Referendum was still just an egregious glint in Nigel Farage's eye). The Rapa Nui are thought to have eventually wiped themselves out in a civil war caused by famine due to all the trees having been destroyed in order to transport the huge quarried stones used to carve the *Moai*; they are used in the poem as idols to desolation after years of austerity and state asset-stripping. **Kraken**: giant sea monster of Norse Mythology. This poem was originally published in a slightly different form in *The Robin Hood Book — Verse Versus Austerity* (2011/12).

RU-RI-TANNIA!
As explained within the poem itself, *Ruritannia* is an amalgam of 'Rule Britannia', and Ruritania, the antiquated Central European kingdom in Anthony Hope's uchronian romance, *The Prisoner of Zenda* (1894), and its sequel, *Rupert of Hentzau* (1998). Napoleon Bonaparte (1769-1821) was disparagingly nicknamed 'the **Little Corporal**'. **a race of shopkeepers**: The phrase was first used in an offensive sense by the French revolutionary Bertrand Barère de Vieuzac on 11 June 1794 in a speech to the National Convention: "Let Pitt then boast of his victory to his nation of shopkeepers", but it was later ascribed to Napoleon. **Bognor Riga**: the seaside town of Bognor Regis in West Sussex has a very large population of Eastern Europeans, mostly Polish, Lithuanians, Latvians (hence Riga, Latvia's capital) and Estonians. **trump trump trump** is from *'Nellie the Elephant packed her trunk And said goodbye to the circus Off she went with a trumpety-trump Trump, trump, trump'*, a 1956 children's song by Ralph Butler. **The Duchy of Grand Fenwick** *see* Notes to **Not Paternoster Square** above. **We might lose our rainbows but we'll keep our unicorns!** alludes to the phrase *'unicorns and rainbows'* which means a dreamy state of bliss usually used sarcastically to describe a desired end as improbable or impractical. But *'unicorns'* has also become a term used to describe unrealistic expectations from Brexit —in the context of this line of the poem, then, **rainbows** might

be interpreted as representing multiculturalism and cosmopolitanism. **Mote in the Beam-end**: allusion to both the slang phrase *'beam ends'* meaning the rear of someone or something, derived from a nautical phrase, and the 'The Mote and the Beam' parable of Jesus given in the Sermon on the Mount[1] in the Gospel of Matthew, chapter 7, verses 1 to 5. **Boris Greenback, and Baron**: allusion to Baron Greenback, the cupiditous toad villain in the *Danger Mouse* cartoon (1981); a *'greenback'* is also American slang for the dollar note. **Noggin the Nogg**: a popular British children's character who is King of the Northmen (i.e. Norsemen/ Vikings) appearing in his own TV series (of the same name, originally broadcast 1959–1965 and 1979–1980) and series of illustrated books (published 1965–1977), created by Oliver Postgate and Peter Firmin.

Drain the Swamp
It's not popularly known that still highly fashionable brand **Hugo Boss** designed the original Nazi uniforms in the 1930s.

The Pigeon Spikes
Not so much a 'hand up' as a spike up That place where the sun don't shine! is my playing on the popular strapline, *'A hand up, not a hand out'*, adopted by the *Big Issue* in the early days of austerity and apparently pandering to Tory and red top-spun stigmatisation against welfare benefits as perceived unconditional *'handouts'*; disturbingly, the same trope is now used by the Salvation Army, amongst other charitable organisations, and shows how some turns of phrase can rapidly become judgemental memes.

Kipling Buildings
The name of the building in which I underwent an intrusive and traumatic assessment for Personal Independence Payment, which I predictably failed to be awarded on bogus grounds, brought to mind Rudyard Kipling's famous poem of human fortitude, 'If', the opening line of which I couldn't resist pastiching: *'If you can keep your head [PIP] when all about are losing theirs'*. **Pyrrhic victory**: a victory which takes such a toll on the victor that it might as well have been a defeat; named from one such bitter victory in the Pyrrhic War (280-75 BC). The poem went on to joint-win the 2018 Bread & Roses Poetry Award, so at least something positive came out of the circumstances of its inception.

Rudyard Digs
Rudyard here is a pun on the slightly antiquated phrase *'ruddy hard'*, and the Mockney sing-song ballad structure is a Kipling-pastiche in the vein of John Davidson's 'Thirty Bob a Week' (1894).

The Bricks of Henrietta Street
The Bricks of the title refers to the rather austerely designed red hardbacks and orange paperbacks produced for Left Book Club members between 1936 and 1948, all of which bore 'NOT FOR SALE TO THE PUBLIC' on their front covers); Henrietta Street was the London address of LBC publishers Victor Gollancz. **Uchronian**: of or relating to a fictional time period or alternate history. *'fascism*

of the shires': I'd thought I'd picked this phrase up from a newspaper column discussing the rise of Ukip or some such subject, however, on Googling it and only finding references to the 'Scouring of the Shire' chapter towards the end of J.R.R. Tolkien's *Return of the King*, I decided it must have been my own coinage —but the Tolkien association is serendipitous.

Shabby Gentile

The term **Shabby Gentile**, or semineologism, *Shabbigentile*, is a pun on the phrase *shabby-genteel: adj. preserving or aspiring to the forms and manners of gentility despite appearing shabby* (Collins dictionary); something often associated with the aspirant lower-middle class/petit-bourgeois of particularly the late Victorian/Edwardian eras, typified by the character Wilkins Micawber, an impecunious, down-at-heel clerk in Charles Dickens' *David Copperfield* (1850), or George and Weedon Grossmiths' Charles Pooter in *The Diary of a Nobody* (188-9). But the term is subversive, replacing 'genteel' with 'gentile', perennial ethnonym for 'non-Jewish', but in this respect meant almost specifically to denote Christians, particularly those who don't live or think by the Christian principles they claim to represent, and a tacit form of anti-Semitism might be part of that.

The neologism of **Shabbigentile**, is meant to be how the average Shabby Gentile gabbles it, and is also, in its use of an 'i' instead of 'y', suggestive, rather ironically, of 'rabbi'. It is deployed as a noun to depict a kind of macro-personification of what I perceive to be the worst and most tribal traits of the Brexit-voting white English of both the lower-middle- and upper-working classes. For the purposes of the book's title, I decided to amalgamate the two words 'shabby' and 'gentile' into one portmanteau —as opposed to presenting them as two separate words, or hyphenated— as if suggestive of some kind of anti-brand. For a while I toyed with various presentations of this title, at one point setting it out in direct reference to the term 'shabby-genteel' as *Shabby-gentile*, and then *Shabby-Gentile*, which was in part informed by H.G. Wells' beguilingly titled *Tono-Bungay* (1909). Any titular similarity to Howard Spring's *Shabby Tiger* (1934) is unconscious, though both books share themes of austerity.

Why the emphasis on the dichotomy of Jew and Gentile? The elucidation comes more explicitly in a number of other poems in this collection. For those reasons, the term then seemed inevitable for the title of the whole collection. This poem attempts to impeach that self-defeating species, the working-class Tory, or 'blue collar Conservative', particularly 'Essex/new consumer man' and all those smitten with Thatcherism, who debatably betrayed themselves for ephemeral material gains (though the prime one of these, home ownership, or the hope of it, is a temptation almost impossible to resist). But the poem also criticises the upper-working- and lower-middle- shopkeeper and desk job classes. Shabby Gentile's bay window is like a shop display. Visceral, materially acquisitive and anti-intellectual, Shabby Gentile is a mythological amalgam, and in some respects could be counted as a direct descendant of the eponymous hedonist in T.S. Eliot's 'Sweeney Among the Nightingales'.

I'm from a shabby-genteel background myself, lapsed middle-class, or '*skidders*' as sociologists might term us, but there is undoubtedly a danger that my poem might come across as socially judgemental, or even as snobbish. As a socialist, that is not my intention, obviously. The poem mentions Robert Tressell and it is very much in the vein of his socialist criticism of some aspects to working-class culture, such as traditionalism, deference to 'betters', philistinism, and defeatism, that this poem is intended. There are references to fictional working-class autodidacts: socialist signwriter **Frank Owen** from Tressell's *The Ragged Trousered Philanthropists* (1914); the eponymous blue-collar self-taught writer from Jack London's *Martin Eden* (1909); the tormented merchant navy man of Joseph Conrad's *Lord Jim* (1900); and **Jude** Fawley, doomed stonemason-cum-Classical audtodidact of Thomas Hardy's *Jude the Obscure* (1895).

'*long shadows over county grounds, warm beer, invincible green suburbs, dog lovers and pools fillers*' might have come from the pen of John Betjeman but it was actually a rhetorical flourish in a speech by John Major to the Conservative Group for Europe on 22 April 1993. **he needs a light to lighten** is a play on the biblical phrase 'a light to lighten the Gentiles' (Luke 2:32), which is interpreted as meaning salvation or to *en*lighten them. **Anxious corporal**: Arthur Koestler's phrase for self-educating lower rankers in the wartime army. **Benthamites**: after Jeremy Bentham (1747-1832), philosopher, social reformer and founder of Utilitarianism. **Peter Bazalgette**: television executive responsible for much of the British reality TV revolution of the late 90s and Noughties, most heinously, for adapting the egregious *Big Brother* from Holland; his having foisted such televisual effluence on us is deeply ironic in light of his famous great-great-grandfather, Victorian civil engineer Joseph Bazalgatte, who, as chief engineer of London's Metropolitan Board of Works, responded to the 'Great Stink' of 1858 by creating central London's first sewer network. François-René, vicomte de **Chateaubriand** (1768-1848), was a writer, historian, politician credited with founding French Romanticism, hence used here as a figure of high culture by way of contrast. **Paul Dacre**: former editor of the *Daily Mail*, notorious for his reactionary editorship, his **Scabrous Brand** being DMG Media, publishers of the *Mail, Mail on Sunday* and *Metro*, of which he is still editor-in-chief.

gammon: disparaging term used today for British white right-wingers. **Tommy Robinson**'s real name is **Stephen Yaxley-Lennon**, but the implication here is that ordinary people are much more likely to relate to him and his cause under his common-sounding nomdeplume than his real double-barrelled Irish name. **Baa-barbarians**: it's conjectured by some historians and etymologists that the Ancient Greek word for foreigners, *barbaroi* (βάρβαροι), our barbarian, derived from the '*bar bar*' babble they heard when listening to foreign non-Greek tongues, hence my playing on this. **No angel in marble, more a thug in gloss**: Conservative prime minister Benjamin Disraeli (1804–1881), also an acclaimed social novelist, and the originator of 'One Nation' Toryism, of whom an obituarist in *The Times* of 18th April 1883 wrote: '...in the inarticulate mass of the English populace he discerned the Conservative workingman as the sculptor perceives the angel prisoned in a block of marble' from which the phrase '*angels in marble*' was born; it was much later adapted for the title of a study on working-class Conservatism, *Angels in Marble: Working Class Conservatives in Urban England* (Robert T. McKenzie, 1968, Heinemann).

The Problem with Jeremy (Jeremy Mixes with the Wrong Kind of Jews)
The absurdity that Corbyn was criticised for spending the Jewish celebration of Seedar with Judas, the implication being that they were the 'wrong kind' of Jews for him to fraternise with. It would seem, then, that pro-Israel or Zionist Jews have a unique licence to be selectively anti-Semitic.

"St. Jude" & the Welfare Jew
This is the key poem to the connundrum of the collection's title, a poem-polemic exposing the complete hypocrisy of right-wing politicians and red top newspapers which routinely employ the tone and lexicon of Thirties eugenicists and Nazis towards the unemployed (i.e. '*scroungers*', '*shirkers*', '*workshy*' et al) and immigrants but have the temerity to defame and slander lifelong antiracist Jeremy Corbyn (a vocal defender of the unemployed, poor and vulnerable) as an anti-Semite simply because he is pro-Palestinian rights and opposed to the oppressive Netanyahu regime in Israel. It was also this poem which spawned the phrase Shabby Gentile —meant here in terms of upper-working-/lower-middle-class red top newspaper reporters and sub-editors. This poem is only ostensibly on the media-hyped *"St. Jude"* storm of 27 and 28 October 2013.

Malthusian: after Thomas Malthus (1766-1834), scholar and cleric whose *An Essay on the Theory of Population* (1798) argued that population growth constantly threatened to overtake the capacity for the earth to sustain such numbers, or to ameliorate mass poverty, and that '*preventative measures*' should be used to cap populations (such as sexual abstinence, reduction in promiscuity, contraception etc.). Malthus's theories went on to influence the late 19th early 20th c. social hygiene movement, the Neo-Malthusians of the Malthusian League (1877-1927), and the eugenics movement of the early to mid-20th century. My use of the term **Mendelists** is a semi-misnomer used here as a euphemism for eugenicists, derived from the founder of genetics, Gregor Mendel (1822-84), a Moravian Catholic friar. **A.N. Wilson**, writer and columnist who splashed an extraordinary attack on the welfare state in his comment piece on the case of Mick Philpott, unemployed benefit-claimant father found guilty in 2012 of causing the deaths of six of his children by an act of arson and a botched rescue attempt which had apparently been designed to depict him heroically. The reprehensible excerpt from a *Daily Express* column by **Janice Atkinson** speaks for itself as to the character of the former Tory and UKIP now independent MP. *Aktion Arbeitsscheu Reich* (**"work-shy Reich"**): name given by the Nazis to the unemployed. **Bruxism**: excessive grinding of the teeth.

Symplegades: rocky islands in Greek Mythology which sporadically crunched together crushing ships passing between them. **Standard & Poor's, and Moodys**: credit rating agencies.

"Swarm": David Cameron on the refugee crisis: *"a swarm of people coming across the Mediterranean, seeking a better life"*. *"benefit tourism"*: risible and disingenuous Tory and Ukip phrase stigmatising economic migrants. **Cumulus Nimbyus**: part pun on cumulus nimbus (a type of cloud) and the acronym "NIMBY" (*"Not In My Back Yard"*). BRITAIN IS OPEN FOR PREJUDICE: play on George Osborne's phrase *"Britain is open for business"*. **Enoch Powell**: (1912-1998), Birmingham-born Tory MP who in 1968 made a notorious speech warning that *"rivers of blood"* would run in Britain if immigration was left to continue unchecked.

The Strangers' Bar: bar in the Palace of Westminster open only to MPs, parliamentary staff and their guests.

Grand Guignol: Le Théâtre du Grand-Guignol, a highly visceral, horrific form of theatre founded in 1894 by Oscar Méténier, which peaked in popularity between the two world wars. **Desmond's Pseudologia** alludes to Richard Desmond's *Daily Express*, pseudologia meaning 'pathological lying'. **Cagliostro**: Count Alessandro di Cagliostro, alias of Giuseppe Balsamo (1743-1795), an Italian magician, mystic and alchemist.

Daily Mailthusian: portmanteau of *Daily Mail* and *Malthusian*. **Rothmere wringer of vicarious Viscounts, Harmsworths**: the Viscounts Rothmere, a dynasty of chairmen of the *Daily Mail* and General Trust plc; Harold Sidney Harmsworth, 1st Viscount Rothermere was responsible for the notorious HURRAH FOR THE BLACKSHIRTS headline of 19th January 1934, in support of Oswald Mosley (1873–1928) and his British Union of Fascists. **Grand Vizier**: autocrat ruler of the Ottoman Empire. *éminence grise: grey eminence*, someone who wields power behind the scenes, unelected, not in public office.

runcible spoon: phrase from Edward Lear's nonsense rhyme 'The Owl and the Pussycat' (1871). **Comrade Ralph**: Ralph Miliband (1924-1994), Marxist scholar and writer and father of Labour's Miliband brothers. Benjamin **Disraeli** (1804-81), Jewish "One Nation" (i.e. paternalist) Tory leader and twice prime minister (1868; 1874–80), also an esteemed social novelist.

Murdochracy alludes to media mogul Rupert Murdoch's disproportionate newspaper power over our 'democracy'. **yellow journalism**: poorly researched, sensationalist journalism.

Salted Caramels
Caxton House is the headquarters of the DWP. **ink can kill as well** is inspired by a phrase spoken by the eponymous protagonist in Trevor Griffiths' *Bill Brand* (1976), a left-wing Labour MP at odds with parliamentary politics, when he describes the bureaucracy of cuts as *"killing with ink"*. At the beginning of Robert Louis Stevenson's *Treasure Island* (1883), **Black Dog** is a pirate who comes to the *Admiral Benbow* inn to confront old shipmate Billy Bones, a lodger there, about a treasure map; the **black spot** is a dark mark on a piece of paper dished out to Billy Bones by Blind Pew, another pirate and old shipmate from Captain Flint's pirate crew, which petrifies recipients and leads directly to Bones' death by stroke. **Reekie, Clapson, Salter**: surnames of three fatalities of the punitive Tory/DWP sanction regime, their tragic fates paid tribute in two poems and the lengthy title poem of my previous collection, *Tan Raptures* (Smokestack Books, 2017).

Chancellor David Lloyd George, 1909 'People's Budget': *"**Four Spectres** haunt the Poor —Old Age, Accident, Sickness and Unemployment. We are going To exorcise them..."*. These were the rhetorical precursors to the *"**Five Giant Evils** of Want, Disease, Squalor, Ignorance and Idleness"* cited in William Beveridge's Report of 1942 which set the template for the Welfare State built under Clement Attlee's Labour Government 1945-51. **Kafkaesque**: anything resembling the writings of Frank Kafka, which were frequently surreal, heavily symbolic, concerned with doom and paranoia and tortuous riddling conspiracies of silence —hence often used today to describe bureaucracies.

Doublespeak is language that deliberately obscures, disguises, distorts, or reverses the meaning of words, sometimes euphemistic; the term and concept originated in George Orwell's dystopian masterpiece *Nineteen Eighty-Four* (1949). **Salted Caramels** was taken out from *Tan Raptures*, along with a number of other poems, partly to reduce its length, but also because, in the case of this poem, I felt the metaphorical motif for brown envelopes of the poem's title might have distracted from or clash with the overarching imagery of that book.

Waiting for Giro
The title is a pun on that of Samuel Beckett's groundbreaking minimalist masterpiece, *Waiting for Godot* (1953). The name **Wragdole** is meant as an amalgam of *"WRAG"* (Work-Related Activity Group, the conditionality group of Employment and Support Allowance) and *'dole'*, that somewhat disparaging term for welfare benefits. **Escrogurn** is an anagram of Scrounger, it also echoes the name Estragon (Gogo), one of the two protagonists in Beckett's play.

Blood of the Dole
Eudemonia: happiness, welfare, human flourishing (Ancient Greek). **Uncle Stanley**: Stanley Baldwin, three times prime minister of the Tory Government (1923-24, 1924-29) and the Tory-led National Government (1935-37) which was pretty much the template for the Tory-led 'Coalition' Government of 2010-15. This poem was inspired by a cutting courtesy of Graham Stevenson's '80 years

ago...' column in the *Morning Star*.

Another Five Giants
fee-fi-fo-fum is from the late 18th/early 19th c. English fairy tale *Jack and the Beanstalk*, the warning song of the Giant:

Fee-fi-fo-fum
I smell the blood of an Englishman:
Be he alive, or be he dead,
I'll grind his bones to make my bread.

Recumbentibus: A knock-out punch —either verbal or physical (from Latin via 'recumbent'). **Bowdlerised**: 'remove material that is considered improper or offensive from (a text or account), especially with the result that the text becomes weaker or less effective' (OED); derived from the surname of Thomas Bowdler, a physician famous for publishing *The Family Shakespeare*, a censored publication of the Bard's *Complete Works*, as well as an expurgated version of Edward Gibbon's *The Decline and Fall of the Roman Empire*, though it was actually his daughter, Henrietta Maria Bowdler, who 'edited' the volumes.

Scroungermongering: my neologism amalgamating the terms Scrounger and scaremongering. **Rough Musickings**: Rough Music, also known as *Charivari* (or *shivaree* or *chivaree*), or *Skimmington*, was a folk custom of mock parades accompanied by raucous improvised noise or music beat out on pots and pans and was aimed at expressing disapproval of those in a community who were perceived to have transgressed behavioural norms, so a kind of figurative vigilanteeism.

Butcher's Apron: derogitory slang-term for the Union Jack, comparing it to the bloodied blue-and-white-striped British butcher's apron, meant to reference the more unscrupulous and brutal colonial exploits of the British Empire. **Agincourt salutes**: euphemism for the twos up finger sign thought to have originated from the V-shaped hand-formations of English longbowmen at the battle of Agincourt (1415) —its inverted version was of course iconically adopted by Winston Churchill for his 'victory' salute.

Ogmagogs: my amalgam of Og, Gog and Magog, names of Satanic Giants prophesied to be confronted and defeated by the Messiah at the end of days, according to the Book of Revelation; the amalgam is also meant to evoke the term *osmagogue*, which means stimulating of the sense of smell. This poem is something of a verse-essay in that it contains as part of its text various lengthy quotes and excerpts from speeches and also includes dates, references and attributions, all of which saves significantly on these Notes.

A.M.

Note on the poet

Alan Morrison is author of several critically acclaimed poetry collections: *The Mansion Gardens* (2006), *A Tapestry of Absent Sitters* (2009), *Keir Hardie Street* (2010), *Captive Dragons/ The Shadow Thorns* (2012), *Blaze a Vanishing/ The Tall Skies* (2013), *Shadows Waltz Haltingly* (2015) and *Tan Raptures* (2017). He is also author of a verse-play, *Picaresque* (2008), and of an epic polemical poem-in-progress, *Odour of Devon Violet* (2014- www.odourofdevonviolet.com).

He is founding editor of socialist literary webzine *The Recusant* (www.the recusant.org.uk) and polemical poetry webzine *Militant Thistles* (www.militant thistles.com). He selected and edited the two pioneering anti-austerity poetry anthologies, *Emergency Verse — Poetry in Defence of the Welfare State* (2011) and *The Robin Hood Book — Verse Versus Austerity* (2012; both Caparison).

His poetry has been awarded grants from the Arts Council, the Royal Literary Fund and the Society of Authors. He was joint winner of the 2018 Bread & Roses Poetry Award. Website: www.alanmorrison.co.uk.

Publications

Recent publications from **Culture Matters**, available from http://www. culturematters.org.uk/index.php/shop-support/our-publications

The Trouble with Monsters by Christopher Norris

Christopher Norris's new collection of political poems takes aim at some monsters of our present bad times, among them Donald Trump, Boris Johnson, Jacob Rees-Mogg, Theresa May, George Osborne, Benjamin Netanyahu, and assorted hangers-on. The satire is unsparing and the dominant tone one of anger mixed with sorrow, compassion and a vivid sense of the evils and suffering brought about by the corruptions of political office.

The influence of Brecht is visible throughout, as is that of W.H. Auden's mordant verse-commentary on politics and culture in the 1930s, along with the great eighteenth-century verse-satirists Dryden, Pope and Swift. Norris leaves the reader in no doubt that we now face a global, European and domestic neo-fascist resurgence.

One of These Dead Places by Jane Burn

One of the voices rarely heard in modern poetry is that of working-class women, in terms of both the impact of major historical events on their identity, health and happiness, as well as their day-to-day experiences of work, men and motherhood.

In this remarkable, powerful collection, Jane Burn has told her story and more, in a series of poems which are both personal and political. She has also illustrated the poems with a beautifully imaginative series of illustrations, which add depth and detail to the collection.

This is a vital collection for our time. Are things worse than the 80s? Have a read, then decide —you won't be disappointed. As one of the titles says: these poems are 'Sentences to Survive In'.

From Aberfan t Grenfell by Mike Jenkins and Alan Perry

From Aberfan t Grenfell shows that Mike Jenkins's sublime skills in dialect poetry continue to shine as brightly as ever, as he evokes a bravura array of voices from his Merthyr bro. Using his work to give speech to people without power, Jenkins's poetry dramatizes the characters and struggles of a community — but also a community's surviving capacity to raise its voices against the power-structures which cause it to suffer. Compassionate and incisive in equal measure, **From Aberfan t Grenfell** is required reading in an era of austerity.

—**Professor Matthew Jarvis**, Anthony Dyson Fellow in Poetry, University of Wales Trinity Saint David

We Will Be Free!
The Bread and Roses Poetry Award Anthology 2018
edited by Mike Quille, with an Introduction by Len McCluskey

The poems all reflected the fact that we find ourselves in such bleak and alienating times — making this type of competition more crucial than ever. And this year we had a particularly healthy number of entries from women and from young people — again, a reflection of deep, unvoiced feelings from those hardest hit, by today's increasingly rampant inequality.

—**Mary Sayer**, a judge of the Bread and Roses Poetry Award

We must take heart from the response in this competition, as well as more widely, that the working class are continuing their fight for justice, equality, and freedom —be it the economic struggle on the picket line, the political struggle through the ballot box, and the cultural struggle through poetry, the arts generally, and other cultural activities.

Society cannot be changed solely from the top, even with a progressive Labour government. It needs strong unions, not an add-on to government but to assist in building the foundations of a more just and equal country. None of this can be done without socialist culture policies—for the many, not the few.

—**Len McCluskey**, General Secretary, Unite

Ruses and Fuses by Fran Lock and Steev Burgess

Fran takes us to the rebellious, inspiring heart of English dissent with her portrayals of Levellers and Diggers such as Gerard Winstanley and Ned Ludd, and their fight with authorities over property rights. She also writes of witches, working-class suffragettes, and the unsung, unlovable labours of working-class women. Her poetry conflates historical detail and present crisis to highlight both the continuation of violence against women, and the continuum of solidarity and sisterhood that exists despite this abuse.

As with her first collection, **Ruses and Fuses** is adorned with the poignant, sensitive collages of Steev Burgess. Together, text and image rail powerfully against neoliberal capitalism and its globalised threat to the livelihoods, health and happiness of working-class people.

Poetry on the Picket Line
an anthology edited by Grim Chip and Mike Quille

Poetry with principles. Poetry with a point. Poetry on the picket line. That's where it should be.
                                                                    —Billy Bragg

Poetry on the Picket Line sounds a bit unlikely, but it works. It's a squad of writers prepared to turn up on picket lines and read poetry. Something a bit different, and it usually goes down well.

The poets do what it says on the tin. They turn up at pickets and demos and read poems —with a mic, without a mic, through a bullhorn, whatever. Pickets are generally pretty pleased and surprised to see them. They appreciate the support, and some of them even appreciate the poetry!

It matters because it brings poetry onto picket lines and picket lines into poetry. Real people connecting with real poetry in the real world. That's got to be a good thing!

This anthology of poems from PotPL is sponsored by trade unions: PCS, RMT and TUC (London, East and South East). All proceeds from the sale of this book will go into strike funds.

arise! by Paul Summers

This pamphlet-length poem celebrates the rich heritage and culture of mining communities, which is expressed so vibrantly and colourfully in the marches, the banners, the music and the speeches at the Durham Miners' Gala. It invokes the collective and co-operative spirit of past generations of men and women who worked and struggled so hard to survive, to build their union, and to organise politically to fight for a better world.

Arise! also celebrates the new, resurgent spirit in the Labour Party, led by Jeremy Corbyn, and the renewal of support for socialist solutions to the country's growing economic and social problems.

It's wonderful to see the proud history of the Durham Miners' Gala represented in this powerful poem. Paul Summers has managed to capture the spirit of the Miners' Gala and its central place in our movement's mission to achieve 'victory for the many, and not the few'.

—**Jeremy Corbyn**, leader of the Labour Party

10% of the proceeds of sales of this book will go to the Durham Miners' Association Redhills Appeal, to help turn Redhills into a cultural hub for the area.

The Combination by Peter Raynard

Peter Raynard has written a remarkable new long poem to mark the 200th anniversary of Marx's birth, and the 170th anniversary of the publication of the Communist Manifesto.

Like the Manifesto, it protests the injustice and exploitation which is integral to capitalism, and the growing gap between capitalism's productive potential and the unequal distribution of its benefits. And like that Manifesto, it is a dynamic and powerful piece of writing —pungent, oppositional and unsettling.

This poetic coupling is something else. It's a re-appropriation, a reclamation, a making sing. It's bolshie (yes, in every sense), provocative and poignant too. It takes the Manifesto back from all that is dead, dry and terminally obfuscated. It's a reminder of reality, the flesh on the theory. It gives Marx to those of us who need him most. Not just relevant, but urgent. Not just angry, but hopeful.

—**Fran Lock**

Power Play by Mair De-Gare Pitt, with images by Jill Powell

From the very first poem this collection focuses on the human and, through its brilliant lyricism, elevates the experiences it describes into something like beauty. The collection understands that the real way to political change is by moving people, by getting hold of their hearts, and by writing memorably, which the poems do again and again.

This collection is wonderfully illustrated by Jill Powell, the images and poems now endorsing each other, now opening each other up to new possibilities of meaning.

I'd say this collection is important because it's political. But I'll say more. It's important if you're human.

—Jonathan Edwards

The Earth and the Stars in the Palm of Our Hand
by Fred Voss

I want to change the world, I want to strike the spark or kick the pebble that will start the fire or the avalanche that will change the world a little.

— Fred Voss

Fred Voss has been a metalworker in workshops in Long Beach, California for over 30 years. His poems are set in the world of work —the workers and bosses in the machine shop where he works, the social usefulness of the products they make, the alienation aggression and camaraderie of the workplace and the relationship of work to the wider world. The poems sympathetically criticise that world, but also envision a better, fairer world, in and out of the workplace.

Everyone can see the growing inequality, the precarious and low paid nature of employment, the housing crisis in our cities, the divisions and inequalities between social classes, the problems of obesity, drink and drugs, and the sheer everyday struggle to pay the bills for many working people.

In this situation, Fred Voss is like a prophet. He is warning us of the consequences of the way we live, he is telling truth to power, and he is inspiring us with a positive vision of a possible—and desirable—socialist future.

—Len McCluskey, General Secretary of Unite

The Things Our Hands Once Stood For by Martin Hayes

Martin Hayes is the only British poet who writes consistently and seriously about work, and about the insanity of a society where employees are seen merely as mere 'hands' to be employed and to make money for their employer.

Work is what most of us have to do, and the workplace is where most of us spend a large part of our lives. Work should be about creatively transforming the world around us to meet all our needs, but it isn't. For the many, work is hard, precarious, poorly paid, unsatisfying and alienating, and constantly threatened by automation. Workers 'never get to share in its profits/but always seem to get to share/in its losses'. Why? Because of the few who own their labour 'squeezing away at people's lives like they were plastic cups'.

The clear message of his poetry is that those who do the work should own, control, and benefit fully from it. They should, in the last words of the last poem, 'start the revolution that will change everything', and show that 'all of our fingertips combined/might just be the fingertips/that keep us and this Universe/stitched together'.

Lugalbanda—Lover of the Seed by Doug Nicholls

Produced as a fundraiser for the Free Ocalan campaign, this new version of a 5,000 year old poem speaks out afresh to our times, with lyrical skill and political relevance.

Lugalbanda, a heroic figure from the Sumerian era, the first civilisation to invent writing, the wheel, law, architecture and irrigation, personifies the amazing creative force at the heart of human culture.

At a time when neoliberal capitalism and its associated ideologies seek to deny and destroy the sense of human agency and labour as the source of all social change, and of all our cultural and material wealth, Lugalbanda reminds us of our deepest, most distinctive social and creative natures, our stupendous power to create and destroy, and the joys of communication and social interaction.

On Fighting On!
The Bread and Roses Poetry Anthology 2017

An anthology of poems from the Bread and Roses Poetry Award 2017, sponsored by Unite.

We sponsored the first Bread and Roses Poetry Award because we believe that our members, and working people generally, have an equal right to join in and enjoy all the arts, and other cultural activities. We believe we should be able to afford them, get to them, and enjoy them, and that art should seek to engage with all sections of the community. Working-class people face a continual cultural struggle to defend our cultural commons, to keep cultural activities open to the many, not the few.

—**Len McCluskey**, General Secretary of Unite

Muses and Bruises by Fran Lock and Steev Burgess

Fran Lock's socialist poetry weaves psychological insight and social awareness into themes of poverty, mental health problems, sexual abuse, domestic violence and political struggle. It is vivid, lavish and punchy, combining a deep sense of anger and injustice with vulnerable empathy and compassion.

The fragmented yet coherent collages of Steev Burgess complement and enhance those meanings perfectly. His images dance with the poems, singing together about muses and bruises, fantasy and reality —grind and grime with a lick of glitter.

A Third Colour by Alan Dunnett and Alix Emery

Through the sheen of vivid, simple narratives and vignettes, we glimpse more disturbing, ambivalent themes of alienation, dislocation and suffering, the psychological fallout of anxiety in modern capitalist culture.

A Third Colour is a book of visionary, poetic parables and dystopian, uneasy images. It is a principled and skilful expression of, and protest against, the world we live in.

Slave Songs and Symphonies
by David Betteridge and Bob Starrett

Slave Songs and Symphonies is an ambitious, beautifully crafted collection of poems, images and epigraphs. It's about human history, progressive art and music, campaigns for political freedom, social justice and peace. Above all it's about the class and cultural struggle of workers 'by hand and by brain' to regain control and ownership of the fruits of their labour.

David Betteridge's poems are leftist, lyrical, and learned, infused with sadness and compassion for the sufferings of our class, the working class. They are also inspired by visionary hope, and a strong belief that our class-divided society and culture can be transformed by radical politics and good art —and by radical art and good politics.

Bob Starrett's drawings are much more than illustrations. They dance with the poems, commenting on them as well as illustrating them. They are like Goya's drawings in their dark, ink-black truthfulness and their intimate knowledge of suffering and Blake's 'mental fight'. Like the poems, they express and resolve the struggles they depict.

Slave Songs and Symphonies tells the story of how slave songs become symphonies —and helps makes it happen. It is not just about class and cultural struggle— it is class and cultural struggle.

Bring the Rising Home! by Mike Jenkins and Gustavius Payne

Weaving through both poems and images are themes of individual isolation and alienation, and the urgent need to recognize that collective action is necessary to change the conditions of working people. Mike Jenkins's vivid, lyrical poems work together with Gustavius Payne's bold, striking, and deeply sympathetic paintings, complementing each other perfectly.

Here is a poetic and painterly union of two socialist Welsh artists who, in their own brilliant, artistic way, are interpreting and changing the world —bringing the Rising home!